Peace — The Roots of the Cultural Tradition and
Values of the Chinese People

Peace — The Roots of the Cultural Tradition and Values of the Chinese People

Wu Genyou

FOREIGN LANGUAGES PRESS

First Edition 2007

Home Page:
http://www.flp.com.cn
E-mail Addresses:
info@flp.com.cn
sales@flp.com.cn

ISBN 978-7-119-04493-4
© Foreign Languages Press, Beijing, China, 2007
Published by Foreign Languages Press
24 Baiwanzhuang Road, Beijing 100037, China
Distributed by China International Book Trading Corporation
35 Chegongzhuang Xilu, Beijing 100044, China
P.O. Box 399, Beijing, China
Printed in the People's Republic of China

CONTENTS

FOREWORD

Zheng He's Fleet and the Road of Peaceful Development of Modern China

More than 600 years ago, on 11th of July, 1405, a grand Chinese fleet left the Liujiagang Port in Suzhou to embark on a voyage through the Yangtze River and out into the Pacific Ocean. This pioneered the greatest oceanic voyage in China's history as well as the history of the world at that time. The fleet contained a number of powerful ships, the largest being 148 meters long and 60 meters wide, with a freight weight of over a thousand tons and the capacity of 1,000 passengers. However, the mission was not one of looking for gold or other treasures, but to preach the benevolent virtue of the emperor of the Ming Dynasty to the island countries of the South Pacific in the hope of achieving a friendly co-existence with them. It was a world of difference from the motivation of Columbus when he sailed the ocean to find wealth across the Atlantic.

Model of one of Zheng He's ships

Today, when China has made remarkable progress in economic development through a hundred years' endeavor, some thinkers and politicians of the West, who look at China's development with a cold war mentality, put forward the idea that "China is a threat." They fear that China's economic development will cause security problems for other countries.

Will China adhere to the road of peaceful development? How are we to comprehend the road of peaceful development put forward by the Chinese government?

To answer these two questions it is necessary to understand the cultural tradition and national virtue of China. China takes the road of peaceful development not merely because it is still a developing country proceeding with a bulk of hard problems to tackle. It will take two or three generations for China to catch up with the medium developed countries. Even by then, China will still be a country that is saying and doing much as it is doing now. Those people who worry "Will China say and do the same as today when she is really powerful?" really have no need to fear.

China is a country that attaches importance to history and historical lessons. In studying the road of China's peaceful development, one should not ignore the influence of the Chinese cultural tradition and its historical and political experience on its current and future political actions. The concept of "valuing harmony" formed in Chinese history and the political experience of the past dynasties in the peaceful handling of relations with the nationalities on its borders will have a profound influence on current and future Chinese politics. Besides the political experience of the Chinese people themselves, the miserable lessons of the two world wars in modern times remain fresh in the minds of the Chinese people. China is listed among the victorious countries in both those world wars, just in name. She never gained any benefit from them.

China has been a country that attaches great importance to fair distribution of wealth and social stability in dealing with the relationships among ethnic groups and with foreign countries. She attaches particular importance to peaceful means in addressing the complicated interactions among different countries. Confucius once said. It is essential to worry more about lack of equality than scarcity and more about unrest than poverty. This cultural concept and attitude toward life has profoundly influenced the Chinese

people's attitude toward wealth. Between the contention for and fair possession of wealth and a peaceful life, the Chinese incline more to peace. In
Chinese history, Gu Danfu, the founder of the Zhou Dynasty, preferred to
cede some of his political territory rather than clash with the Di people, a
minority ethnic group on the northeast border, when he had contradictions
with them. Why was this? Gu said, what the Di people needed was nothing
but the land and the people. It was better to hand them the land and the people and let them manage these rather than to launch a war for the sake of
land and people. It would be the same to the people no matter who ran them.
So he moved the Zhou tribe to the foot of Mount Qi in order to reclaim new
land. Feeling grateful for his benevolence, the people were willing to follow
him to Mount Qi. Therefore, the Zhou Dynasty gradually grew stronger and
stronger. This might be a legendary story about the benevolent political rule
of the Zhou Dynasty, but it shows that China craved for benevolent rule
after the Zhou Dynasty ended.

The Chinese people are used to having a happy life, even though poor.
In the history of the dynasties, some of the rulers would rather spend a great
deal of money for peace at the border than to become engaged in war for the
purpose of achieving peace. A typical example is the fact that in 1004 Emperor Zhao Heng of the Song Dynasty signed an alliance with the Liao State
(the forefathers of Manchu people). Throughout Chinese history, very few
dynasties launched wars against the nationalities at their borders to plunder
for wealth. Emperor Wu of the Han Dynasty (140-86 B.C.) sent troops to
attack the Huns in the north. He waged a war to maintain peace on the border because his policy of "marriage for peace" had proved to be futile. Even
such a war was continually criticized by the intellectuals influenced by
Confucian ideas in the later orthodox history books. This was because it cost
a huge volume of wealth through several wars to drive out the Huns. The
intellectuals believed it was not worth the price by weighing the gains and
losses. In the Chinese traditional thinking of "harmony between man and
nature" it was better not to harm anyone, even wolves or jackals, so long as
they did not harm people. All one should do was to drive them away so as to
ensure safety of people. This concept of self-protection and forgiving
co-habitation made the Chinese unwilling to make enemies of other nations
or to launch wars for wealth.

China is a nation with a long history of an agrarian culture. The development of this culture nourished the idea of "harmony between man and nature," namely, an ecological concept of organic coordination between man and nature and an exclusive mode of medicinal mentality — overall balance in traditional Chinese medicine — formed in the exchange process between man and nature. This mentality still has an important influence on the modern Chinese people.

Among the various ideological trends in the West that spread to China in the late 19th century, the Chinese people finally chose the socialist ideal founded and enriched by Marxists. As the fundamental ideology of the country, it has profoundly regularized the actions of the Chinese people in their modernization drive, that is, taking the international socialist road that is developing along with all the peoples of the world.

The concept of China's peaceful development actually expresses the cultural idea that the Chinese people will take the road of modernization with Chinese characteristics. China now is on the road to modernization. Learning from the lessons and experiences of the modernizations of Western countries in the 19th and 20th centuries, China made a choice for peaceful development, which was wise. The reason why China made such a choice is closely linked with the political wisdom of "worshiping peace" and "valuing harmony" of Chinese traditional culture. Therefore, to further explore the ideological tradition of "valuing harmony" in Chinese culture may deepen the understanding of the profound cultural roots of "China's peaceful development." Such a peaceful development is by no means an expedient political strategy or foreign strategy of the modern Chinese statesmen.

Undoubtedly, the rising of a big country will inevitably bring about changes in the world situation and will affect the distribution of the world's resources. However, the question is whether to use peaceful means to realize redistribution through economic and cultural interactions so as to upgrade the livelihood of the people of the world or to use wars to plunder resources that will bring disastrous consequences for the people of the world. These are two totally different roads used for development of big countries. In the long process of rising and growing of the Chinese nation, China has accumulated rich wisdom in peaceful development. Under many situations, Chinese politicians throughout history were more inclined towards using "marriage for peace" to cope with its relations with nationalities at the borders.

The diplomatic and cultural envoys of the Han (206 B.C.-A.D. 220) and the Tang (618-907) dynasties were sent as envoys of peace to other regions to conduct diplomatic liaisons and cultural exchanges. During the early Ming Dynasty (1368-1644), Zheng He's fleet made seven oceanic voyages in the basic spirit of peace and friendliness to develop diplomatic relations with the countries of Southeast Asia. This became an example of peaceful exchanges before the development of the modern industrial and commercial society. The "Silk Road" was a road of peaceful trade as well as a route by which to peacefully spread culture. Witnessing the aftermath of the calamity of the two world wars, China, in choosing the road to modernization, unswervingly adheres to the international principle of taking the modernization road of peaceful co-existence, friendly neighbors, and common development. Since Deng Xiaoping's policy of opening up and reform, China's economic development in the past 20-odd years has brought about down-to-earth and tangible benefits for the people of the world. During the Asian financial crisis, the Chinese government, as a responsible government for international affairs, made great contributions to the maintenance of regional economic stability by putting international justice as the priority between the choices of international justice and China's national interest. In recent years, on the issue of a nuclear-free Korean Peninsula, the organizing of the six-party talks embodies the efforts of the Chinese government in maintaining regional peace.

When globalization makes "families" of the "global village" closer, China is a part of the Chinese people as well as of the world. Any country attempting to use non-peaceful means to develop its economy will bring disaster to the people of the world as well as its own people. Concurrently, peaceful development is the cultural theme for this time in the world and a historical mission for all mankind. Different nations have their own spirit and tradition of loving peace.

The Chinese nation has a long history of such a tradition. In the long process of civilization, China has learned profound lessons as well as achieved political experience in cherishing a peace-loving spirit. This book aims to show the cultural resources and binding forces of ideals in China's current and future peaceful development through an exploration of the Chinese tradition of peace and through an analysis of the ancient and modern Chinese cultural ideal.

This book will not describe various wars in Chinese history because the descriptions of them are detailed in many historical works. Instead, this book will concentrate on a description of the cultural tradition of the peace-loving Chinese. This does not, however, mean that it intends to describe China as a nation yielding to humiliation in the achievement of peace. In the development and formation of the Chinese nation, in order to maintain territorial integrity and national security, the Chinese have always heroically fought back all aggressors even when their military forces were overwhelmed.

In his important work of *The Ideal State*, Plato, the greatest philosopher of ancient Greece, talked about the wisdom of running a state that he learned from Socrates, a wise man. He held that a state was made up of money-makers, auxiliaries, and intellectuals. The individuals of these three classes had corresponding desires, enthusiasm, and rational thinking. If any individual was able to control their desires and enthusiasm with rational thinking, then that person was a man of justice and virtue. Whenever a state was controlled by the rational class over the other two classes, that state was the one with justice and morals. Thus, following the vision of Plato's wisdom, when a nation is controlled by wisdom over all parts of the nation, that nation has justice and morals. It is, of course, impossible for a nation to have wisdom all the time throughout its long history of development. Sometimes, when those forces representing desire and enthusiasm become dominant, turmoil and wars take place. In passing through the tunnel of history, the Chinese nation has for the most part been able to maintain the force of wisdom over the zealous demands of those representing desire and enthusiasm at the most critical junctures, and the nation was able to overcome many difficulties and hardships, shake off the control of the devil of death, and regain the opportunity of reviving the civilization.

I would like to conclude this Foreword by quoting Zhang Zai, a great ancient thinker who lived from 1020 to 1077. In his work, entitled *On Supreme Harmony* (《太和篇》), he wrote "The great benevolence in the form of supreme harmony includes the natural phenomenon of an interaction of rising and falling, movement and tranquility, which commences with frictions, victories and defeats, and coil and extension in integrity. Their coming into being is flat and simple but their ultimate consequence is broad and solid. The wisdom from the changes is nothing but the heaven while the examples from the simplicity are nothing but the earth. When they spread out, they are the *qi* that can be imitated, while the magical spirit is crystal and smooth that cannot be imitated. It will be called the supreme harmony only when these are mingled and integrated as natural phenomenon."

Chapter I

Ancient Wisdom Pointing
Toward Harmony

"Zai," the first of the two ancient Chinese characters for prime minister, means chef for the king. Chapter one of *The Rites of Zhou* (《周礼》), a book about the record of the ancient political system, describes the position and job functions of the "Supreme Zai" in the imperial palace to show the importance of its coordination of the affairs in the palace in helping the king run state affairs.

1. Soup-cooking and Political Wisdom for
Harmony of the Chinese People

In historical documents of ancient China, there are many stories about how some famous statesmen used the theory of soup-cooking in dealing with contradictions in their political life. These stories amply reflect the political wisdom of the Chinese people, namely, the pursuit after harmony.

(1) "Harmonious as Soup," and "Making up for a Lack, and Releasing the Excessive"

Chinese food is quite popular throughout the world. Why is it so? What is the secret in Chinese food? It has something to do with the idea of harmony

Cooking vessels gradually developed into sacrificial vessels during the Shang and Zhou dynasties.

in Chinese cuisine. As the Chinese saying goes, the harmony of five flavors leads to a hundred delicacies. The Chinese outlook of attaching importance to harmony and coordination can be found in expressions everywhere from the classics to daily life. Some great politicians often used this to elaborate their political principles. For example, as recorded in *Zuo Zhuan* (《左传》, first chronological history covering the period from 722 to 464 B.C.), Yan Zi, a famous prime minister of the State of Qi during the Warring States Period, used cooking to illustrate the situation of political harmony. He said that if one wanted to have a harmonious situation in the midst of different political forces in political life, one needed to learn from the chef in cooking soup. The chef used fire, water, sauce, salt, and plum sauce to marinate fish or meat, then gradually heated this up to simmer so that the flavors of the soup interacted and inter-penetrated with aim of letting each part "make up for what was lacking and to release the excessive." Finally the fresh and delicate soup was made.

Many successful kings and emperors in history executed their power in this way, like making soup with a harmony of the tastes of sour, sweet, bitter, spicy, and salty, or like an orchestra producing philharmonic music by combining five tones. The metaphor was used to advise people in power to keep a peaceful and calm mentality in pursuit after an objective and a fair method in addressing problems to fulfill the ultimate political mission.

Yan Zi further elaborated that, in political activities, it was essential not to be afraid of differences or even contradictory factors or matters. Political action was applied to coordinate differences and contradictions so as to show the value and function of political actions. If one adds water to boiled water, one can never make delicious soup no matter how long the water cooks. Political activities were for the purpose of coordinating different demands and requests of all the people.

During the sixth century B.C., Liang Qiuju, a favorite minister of the Duke Jing of the State of Qi, was especially adept at satisfying all kinds of likes of the Duke. One day Duke Jing told Yan Zi that Liang had a very harmonious relation with himself. Yan Zi immediately replied that the relationship between Liang and the Duke was not harmonious, but exactly the same. "He particularly curries favor to your likes, and this is not harmony at all."

Confucius, the great thinker of the State of Lu in the same period, later put forward the principle of "harmony with differences." This principle has had a deep historical influence both on the development of Chinese personalities and modern Chinese policies and on foreign affairs in upholding international rules and forging an independent foreign policy.

Yan Zi, as one of the greatest politicians of the State of Qi, carried out the political wisdom of valuing and making use of harmony in all his political activities. When he was sent as an envoy to the State of Chu, the people of Chu disparaged him because they saw him as being short, fat and dark. So they only opened a side gate for him. As the envoy of the State of Qi, a powerful state at that time, Yan Zi did not want to see this as the humiliation of his state nor did he wish to cause contradictions between the two states. With superior wisdom, he told the gate-keeper of the State of Chu, "I am the envoy from the State of Qi, and I will enter the gate for a dog if I come to the State of dog. But if I come to the State of people, I must enter the front gate." So the gatekeeper had to open the front gate to let Yan Zi and his entourage enter.

When the Duke of Chu met Yan Zi, he noticed that Yan did not look outstanding, so he intended to humiliate him. The Duke said that it seemed the State of Qi lacked men. Figuring out what was behind the Duke's remark, Yan replied that the State of Qi had so many people there would be shade if they all raised their sleeves and there would be rain if they all shed their sweat. Then the Duke asked, "If the State of Qi has so many people, why did it send a person like you as an envoy?" Yan Zi answered back, "The State of Qi has a principle for its foreign affairs. It would send an envoy of virtue to a state of virtue and an envoy of less virtue and talent to a state of less intelligence. I am the least talented, so I was sent to your state." These words put the Duke in an awkward position. But he did not want to let him off like this, so he decided to humiliate him once more. At the official reception, the Duke had two criminals brought into the room. He then intentionally asked the captors, "What crimes have these two committed?" The answer was that they had committed theft. The Duke then asked which state they came from. The answer was that they came from the State of Qi. The Duke turned to Yan Zi, and said, "It seems that people from the State of Qi can only steal, is that so?" Yan Zi immediately stood up and answered, "I have learned that orange trees bear oranges in the south, but when transplanted in the north, they bear something that looks like an orange but it is bitter inside. Why is this? It is because of the changes in soil conditions and climate. These two people observed the law when they were in the State of Qi. They turned into criminals only when they came to the State of Chu. Is that because the situation in the State of Chu favors the nurturing of thieves?" Hearing Yan Zi's answers, the Duke admittedly agreed that it was no fun to joke with the saint because it would only end in bitter humiliation of his own making. As an envoy, Yan Zi used clever diplomatic language to protect the image of his state as well as to fulfill his diplomatic mission of maintaining peace between the two states.

Yan Zi made use of his wisdom in external affairs to gain peace between two powerful states as much as he did in internal affairs. He served as prime minister for three Dukes of the State of Qi. He did his utmost to halt any improper ideas of the Dukes adroitly, politely, and effectively. Duke Jing of the State of Qi was fond of success and had grandiose ideas. He wanted to follow his forefather, Duke Huan of Qi, in having hegemony over everyone. One day he told Yan Zi that he wanted to attack the State of Lu. Yan Zi did his best to dissuade him by saying that the Duke of Lu worshiped morality and that the people loved him. Yan Zi told him that the state that worshiped morality was stable and the state the people loved was at peace. To attack such a state meant putting oneself in an aggressive position. "If you want other states to yield to you," Yan Zi said, "you must keep your own state stable with virtue and have a state policy that ensures people to have a harmonious life. Then it may be possible to send a punitive expedition against tyranny." Through this persuasion by Yan Zi, Duke Jing of Qi gave up his desire to attack the State of Lu.

Yan Zi was a great and modest politician. He always showed modesty whenever he went out in a carriage. One day, the wife of the horseman of Yan Zi peered through her house gate to view the modest and honest manners of Yan Zi, and she was moved. Meanwhile, she saw her husband as being arrogant, self-satisfied, and presumptuous. When her husband came home, she said to him, "Yan Zi stands no higher than 1.6 meters but serves as the prime minister of the State of Qi and is well known among all the states. But, today I saw him in the carriage with calm, quiet manners and high aspiration as well as being modest. However, you are as tall as 1.9 meters but serve as a horseman. It does not matter being a horseman as much as it does being content. I tell you this to prevent an unpredictable mishap." Because of his wife's words, he then became a modest person. One day, he told Yan Zi every word his wife had said to him. Yan Zi considered that this horseman could listen and learn, so he recommended him to become a high official in the State of Qi.

Throughout Chinese history there have been many politicians who have understood and valued harmony as did Yan Zi. The dialogue between Duke Huan of the State of Zheng and Shi Bo illustrates the political benefits of "valuing harmony" from a different angle.

(2) "Harmony Generates Substance; the Identical Finds No Continuity"

During the Spring and Autumn Period (770-476 B.C.), Duke Huan and his Minister Shi Bo were one day discussing the political mistakes of the Zhou Dynasty. Shi Bo said that Emperor You of the Zhou Dynasty was wrong in not listening to different political opinions. In his execution of power, he adopted the erroneous method of discarding harmony but retaining that which was identical with what had gone on before, leading to misunderstanding. This led to the decline of the Zhou Dynasty. Shi Bo profoundly dwelled on the value of harmony and the difference between it and identical views. His view was that only harmony generated all substances, while the identical found no continuity.

Then what is harmony? Shi Bo held that harmony meant that each different thing fell into its place in coordination with each other by getting rid of the differences, surplus, and making up for what was lacking so that everything was something of its own but in a unified and harmonious body. He cited an example of the god who made gold, wood, water, fire, and soil mingle together to creat all things. He went on with more examples. For instance, to harmonize the tastes of sour, bitter, sweet, spicy, and salty to meet man's taste results in good health and a strong body; to use six instruments to set the basic tones for the creation of fine music; to foster the noble soul of a man by correcting the desires of the seven sensory organs; to develop mankind through harnessing heaven, earth, water, fire, thunder, lightening, mountains, wind, and rivers; to establish pure political morals through good administration of six materials, namely water, wood, metal, fire, earth and grain, and three matters, namely upholding virtue, being helpful to utility and giving emphasis on livelihood; and to teach all officials about how to bring together the different casts of ten classes. In the meantime, it is necessary to produce tens of thousands of different kinds of goods, to deal with all

kinds of problems, and to ponder over millions of matters. Therefore, in order to run everything and let the people live a worry free life, the king in the vast land must coordinate the co-existence of all different things, even contradictory things, and try to avoid the pursuit after being identical. Why? It is because only one sound will not make enjoyable music; only one taste will not produce a delicacy; and only one view will leave nothing for discussion.

The viewpoint of Shi Bo showed that the outstanding politicians of ancient China were good at listening to different opinions. The demand

Chime bell is the symbol of the ritual music culture in ancient China, whose structure and sounding effect both represent the character of "harmony."

for only one voice in political life will inevitably lead to the fall of a state. Only by finding the crux of the problem and formulating correct measures to address it will a ruler be able to develop a genuine and harmonious social environment.

Ancient Chinese philosophers particularly liked to cite music as examples to illustrate the importance of harmony in discussing political matters. According to a story in the *Zuo Zhuan*, Duke Jing of Zhuo forged a big bell with an extremely loud sound. Zhou Jiu, a musical official, then asked the Duke, do you want people to die of disease? Music is used by the son of heaven to coordinate amongst all the people. Sounds are the carriage of music while a bell is used for producing sound. Bells and the sound of bells are tools used to educate. Small musical instruments should avoid making too soft a sound because this will not move people, while big musical instruments should avoid making too loud a sound because this will make people feel uneasy. Only when the smaller instruments do not produce soft sounds and the bigger ones do not produce noises, will the music be harmonious. Therefore, a harmonious melody will pass through the hearing senses to the hearts of the people who will derive enjoyment from it. When either the sound is too light or too loud, people will feel uneasy. And they will become ill if they are upset. Now if the bell is made too big and with too loud a sound, Your Excellency can not bear to listen to it for very long. Therefore, how can people bear listening to it for long?

Remarks of Monarchs (《国语》, history of late Western Zhou and major states in the Spring and Autumn Period）has a more detailed record of Zhou Jiu's elaborations on the relations between music and politics. Zhou said, "Political actions are just like music, which follows the principle of harmony just as politics follows the principle of security and safety. Sound tunes the music while tones tune the sound." The supreme principle of harmony is that a big bell produces a magnificent sound while small ones produce a clear sound. Harmony and peace will last long and a longer peace will lead to purity, which results in achievements that will have lasting appreciation. The political situation of benevolent rule is thus developed. That is why our forefather kings cherished musical harmony. If the kings had liked music either too soft or too loud, it would not be of benefit in training people's aesthetic conceptions of harmony. Therefore, it would not be conducive to social harmony. Zhou Jiu shared similar views with Shi Bo: Only when there is a harmonious musical theme will there be lasting prosperity and growing wealth. The fact that Zhou Jiu elaborated the political doctrine of valuing harmony through musical principles was followed by Xun Zi, who discussed political harmony with music theories. They manifested the political wisdom of Chinese ancient politicians and thinkers who were good at deriving political theories from daily life.

Zhou Jiu advised Duke Jing of Zhou mainly from the angle that music should be harmonious in the hope that the Duke would be frugal and show his benevolence to his people rather than show his power through the bell sound. However, the Duke did not accept the musical official's advice. The Duke died in 520 B.C., the second year after the completion of the bell.

(3) "Harmony with Differences"

Confucius (551-479 B.C.), the great thinker of the State of Lu, theoretically elaborated the value of harmony. He explicitly put forth the principle for man's behavior and politics to be in harmony with differences, and he combined the political ideology of harmony with a ritual system. Thus he imbued the ideology of political harmony with an extensive significance.

Confucius

In the Confucian view, the principle for men was harmony with differences and those referred to as gentlemen were the political elite with good education who could assist the king in ruling the state. They had political virtues as well as capabilities. No matter whether they were in an official position or lived an ordinary life, they could coordinate with the people around them but did not follow them with common views or actions.

Confucius said, "Gentlemen harmoniously cohabitate with others but do not follow suit, while lesser men follow suit but do not live harmoniously with others." He also said, "Gentlemen get along with others but do not form a clique, while lesser men form a clique but cannot not get along with others."

With a view to further explaining the difference between harmony and identity, Confucius emphasized the principle of harmony. Though his rites marked the differences between classes, their practical function was to co-ordinate the relationship among the different social classes. The kings of ancient times all pursued harmonious social relations as the highest political ideal. So everything was meant to follow the requirements of the rites. To seek after yes-men for the sake of harmony regardless of the principle of rites in everyday life was unacceptable. When political ideology in pursuit of the goal of harmony was in contradiction with the reality of harmony, Confucius inclined more toward the maintenance of the dignity of rites and opposed harmony without principle. For him, the opposition against harmony without principle meant an opposition against the pursuit of identity. This was in line with Yan Zi's criticism of Duke Qing of Qi. But the difference was that Yan Zi, as a politician, analyzed the difference between harmony and identity with concrete examples, while Confucius theoretically elaborated the principle of realizing political harmony.

In political management, Confucius advocated a combination of soft and hard tactics so as to reach political harmony. According to the "Twentieth Year of Duke Zhao" of *Zuo Zhuan*, Zi Chan, a famous prime minister of the State of Zheng, while lying on his death bed, advised his successor Zi Pi, "You will be taking up my job after I have passed away. Remember that people have fear of fire when they see it from afar, so very few people die in a fire. But water looks soft and people disparage it, so many people unconsciously fall into the water and are drowned." Nevertheless, Zi Pi failed to fully comprehend the meaning of this last will. In pursuit of a reputation of being a lenient prime minister, Zi Pi was too lenient, and thieves and bandits ran amok in the State of Zheng. Zi Pi then regretted his failure to understand the last wishes of Zi Chan that resulted in his harming the people. So he led an army to attack the bandits. It was said that when Confucius learned of the remorse of Zi Pi, he said, "Excellent. Under too lenient policies, the people will relax and it is essential to use hard and powerful measures to correct the situation when people become relaxed. After the implementation of hard policies, people's livelihood may whither and then one should carry out lenient policies. Benevolent policies may relieve the shortcomings brought about by hard policies, while hard policies may remedy the errors of soft policies. Thus a harmonious political situation may be reached."

Zi Si (483-402 B.C.), another great thinker of the Spring and Autumn Period, deemed harmony to be the highest form of political life. In his book, *Doctrine of the Mean* (《中庸》), he wrote: When people have not shown their feelings, this is regarded as being in the middle. When the feelings are expressed in line with rites and reason, this is called harmony. The middle is where everything starts while harmony is the flat path toward the success of everything. If man's action reaches both the middle and harmony, everything will fall into place and everything will be nurtured and developed. This greatly emphasizes the harmonious and orderly environment as a precondition for the development of everything and affirms the significance of the overall environment for the normal development of all things. Therefore, the ideology of middle and harmony, expressed in the *Doctrine of the Mean*, highlighted the importance of the overall environment and harmony not as a measure but as a necessary prerequisite for normal development.

Mencius (372-289 B.C.), one of the most important figures of the Confucian school, developed the concept of human unity in the field of politics. He deemed that "for defense in warfare the favorable weather is not as important as the topographical advantage, and the topographical advantage is not as important as the human unity." Mencius lived during the Warring States Period (475-221 B.C.) and witnessed the rising and falling of states. He summed up a profound principle of politics: In the process of the rising and falling of a state, the changes of natural weather are not as important as the geological terrain. The topographical advantage is not as important as the social unity of the state. In some states, the city wall was high, the moat deep, weapons sharp, and reserves of grain sufficient, but they still could not resist the attacks from enemy states because the soldiers assigned to guard the city fled. This drove home the point that the topographical advantage was not as important as human unity. Therefore, in wars, the unity of the people of a nation is the guarantee of a final victory to the war.

How is one to attain the political goal of human unity? Mencius believed that the ruler must implement benevolent governance. His motto was: Treat the aged parents of others as you would treat your own parents; treat the children of others as you would treat your own children. In this way it will be easy to handle all things, even though the world is big and has all kinds of things.

(4) "Difference Defined by Righteousness Leads to Harmony, Which Leads to Unity," Much Unity Leads to Power and Prosperity

In the later period of the Warring States Period, Xun Zi (313-238 B.C.), a great man of the Confucian school, illustrated the importance of the theory of human unity from various angles. Having inherited the thoughts of Confucius, he recognized the relationship between observing rites and social harmony, and he further adhered to the principles of the classification of rites for the purpose of social harmony. Thus he said that when a ruler worships the principle of rites with the classification of nobles and commoners so as to bring into play all the people of different social statuses, all the different classes will do their part. Scholars will respect the ruler and be loyal to the ritual system; officials will follow the rules and requirements in fear of violating the law; businessmen will be honest without cheating; all workers will work with diligence to produce utensils of good quality; and farmers will be simple in their desires and work hard in farming the fields. Thus the ruler can attain his goal: From above, he will have favorable weather; from below, he will have topographical advantage; and from between, he will have human unity. And everything will thrive. If a ruler can have favorable weather, the topographical advantages, and human unity all at the same time, every person under him will do his utmost. So every order will be carried out, everybody will be happy, and gentlemen will live an easy life, developing their virtue and reputations. Xun Zi aptly affirmed the positive impact and value of social harmony in the daily life of ordinary people and for the elites who wished to achieve merit.

Xun Zi further made an analysis of the difference between man and other species in the world, and in particular an analysis of how mankind could make use of animals. Thus he theoretically exposed the differences in human harmony from the primitive harmony of nature. He said, water and fire have energy but they are not alive, plants and grass are alive but without awareness. Animals and poultry have awareness but without principles of ethics. Man has energy, vitality, awareness, and principles of ethics, so man is the most valuable of all in nature. Man is not as strong as an ox, neither does he run as fast as a horse, but why is it that an ox and a horse are driven by men? It is because men are united. Why can men be united? It is because men can tell the differences from one another and men can universally accept the differences and there are the principles of ethics. The differences between men are formed through the principles of ethics and then reach the harmonious sphere. Harmony on the new sphere will reach a new unity. The unity will generate gigantic social power that will grow strong and thrive. When man is strong he will be able to defeat the objects of nature. That is why man is able to build things like palaces and differs his life from that of animals.

Xun Zi, like Confucius, was a well-educated scholar of arts. He attached great importance to the role that music played in promoting social harmony. Confucius once criticized the music of the State of Zheng. In the late years of the Spring and Autumn Period, the State of Zheng and the State of Wei were both small states and existed between the big states of Qi, Chu, and Wei, but their commercial economy was relatively developed and their folk music was popular. In today's view, the pop music of the State of Zheng, particularly the songs of the expression of love between a man and a woman, were great hits. To Confucius, this kind of music let people's feelings run rampant at the cost of losing harmony. So he wrote off the music of the State of Zheng from the realm of education for ritual music. Of course this showed a narrow-minded understanding of the value of music by Confucius. However, we should not be too harsh on the ancient man. Confucius, dedicated to a political ideal throughout his whole life, was mainly concerned about the practice of ruling so he emphasized the social function of music in achieving social unity.

Xun Zi believed that the ruler and his ministers might enjoy a good song, as would father and his children of a family, farmers of the same village, and so a good song could develop an atmosphere of harmony and mutual respect. Therefore, the art of music was exclusive in its dedication to the principle of unity to maintain harmony through the coordination of playing different musical instruments and through the mix of different tones.

Xun Zi also believed that different forms of music impacted the psychology of people differently. Themes of music would lead to harmony instead of running wild; solid music would lead people to union without disturbance. When people united as one, the troop of a state would be powerful, the defence would be solid, and an enemy state would be refrain from attacking. It was because music had such gigantic social impact that the Confucian scholars advised making the best use of music in political activities so as to achieve a fine political effect of harmonious co-existence through benevolence directed toward the hearts of the people. In the political philosophy of Xun Zi, the status of ancient religion as the manager of the souls of people was declining while his ideal of music was replacing it instead. Cai Yuanpei, a great Chinese educator of the early 20th century, once put forward a concept of "replacing religion with the education of aesthetics," which was actually a form of expressing the classic political philosophy of Xun Zi.

2. Accord of All States

Collection of Ancient Texts (《尚书》)，the earliest Chinese book of history, has many pages on how rulers should maintain harmony in political activities. The character "harmony" appears many times in the book, as do other characters expressing the same idea.

(1) Accord of All States — Concept of Valuing Harmony in the *Collection of Ancient Texts*

Collection of Ancient Texts is full of wisdom in the pursuit of harmony by a state and among all states. For example, when Yao was in power, in order to spread his virtue of benevolent rule, he first ordered all his relatives to live in harmony so as to keep fine relationships that could be emulated by the common people, thus creating orderly human relations in society.

As known to all, the dynasty of Zhou was a federal union of states ruled by dukes. So the supreme leader of the dynasty had to deal with the relations between the states and the relations of the dukes with the Zhou imperial court.

As mentioned before, Yan Zi, the great politician of the State of Qi, made use of the metaphor of cooking soup to illustrate the truth of political harmony.

The Rites of Zhou says that the prime minister had six routine jobs, one of which was to assist the dukes in maintaining harmony within the state and the friendly co-inhabitance of the people.

Lord Zhou Gong, regent of the Zhou Dynasty, told the young King Cheng it was essential to learn from the valuable experience of the forefathers' political practice. He said that when Wuding succeeded the throne, he was faced with a declining situation. He worked hard without saying any unneeded words for three years. Then, when he started to talk freely, the situation under his rule was smooth and peaceful.

When King Wen was in power, he routinely pondered from morning till evening over how to harmonize the people. King Cheng reprimanded people of the fallen Yin Dynasty calling on them to observe the political rites of Zhou but not to stir up trouble and make disturbances or they would be punished. King Cheng said, "You should not create a disturbing situation, but keep harmony as the goal. Your family should be in harmony, which is the goal." He warned some trouble makers, "If you stick to making disturbances, I will surely punish you and you must not bear grievances against me." On his death bed, King Cheng entrusted his throne to Prince Kang, saying, "You shoulder the mission of carrying on the glory of the Zhou Dynasty. I instruct you to succeed to the throne and remember the teachings of our forefathers in leading the Zhou Dynasty, following the laws made by them, and coordinating the harmony of all the people so as to show your gratitude to the glory of the virtue of King Wen and King Wu."

Deng Xiaoping, the architect of the opening-up and reform in China, once said about the political situation, "Stability supersedes everything." Stability in modern Chinese language contains the meaning of harmony and stability. The ancient political wisdom of harmony generates substance and finds its vitality in modern language. The ideal of constructing a harmonious society put forth by the current Chinese government demonstrates the revival of the classic political wisdom of ancient China.

(2) Governance with Virtue

The accord of all states was the political goal of any emperor in handling relations among the states, while the fundamental means was the exercise of governance with virtue, a political principle commonly observed by great rulers Yao, Shun, and Yu of the Xia Dynasty, the first dynasty in China. Though the rulers of the Zhou Dynasty believed that imperial power was preordained by heaven, they understood that they must rely on the virtue of the ruler to keep the preordination. *Collection of Ancient Texts* is replete with references to the ideological inclination toward governance with virtue. The supreme ruler could only have tranquility and harmony through his own fine personal virtue.

That the supreme ruler should possess "fine virtue" was everywhere stated in the *Collection of Ancient Texts*. Yao and Shun, two great rulers in ancient China, did their utmost to win esteem through virtuous governance. In extolling Yao, the "Chapter on Yao" says, "He endeavored to show his fine virtue in the hope that the people of all nine clans would have mutual respect and live in harmony. The people of the nine clans finally reached harmony under the aspirations of his fine virtue." When Yao was at an advanced age, he prepared to turn over his throne to a leader named Siyue, who declined on account of the fact that he was humble and his virtue was not up to the standards of that of the ruler. He recommended Shun as the one to succeed to the throne because he had noble virtues. His arguments were that Shun's father was blind and dull and that his mother not intelligent while his younger brother was arrogant, but Shun respected his parents and was all the more filial because of this and lived harmoniously with his brother. Gao Tao, a justice official under Shun, said that only when one indeed proceeds from his virtue will his tactics and strategy bring about a harmonious effect. Gao Tao wrote about nine different aspects of virtue. He said that the supreme leader should show three virtues every day and keep a sober mind until night and manage his family well. And if he will show six virtues every day, he will run the state well.

Cheng Tang, the founder of Shang Dynasty, saw that King Jie of the Xia Dynasty was lacking virtue and so Cheng Tang led a rebellion to take over power. At the time, he declared, "The king of Xia has exhausted the recourses of the people, deprived them of their harvests, and there were disputes among them. They hate Jie of Xia by complaining that they were willing to die together with the sun if the burning sun would perish. The Xia Dynasty is declining with no virtue. Now I will go on an expedition against him. You should assist me and I will reward you."

In persuading his ministers to move the capital, King Pan Geng said, "It is not me who has lost the fine virtue to rule but it is you who have presumed to have virtue. If you can overcome your selfishness and give substantial benefits to the people, then you might be qualified to declare that you have virtue." Pan Geng reproached his ministers saying, "One should not selfishly collect wealth but rather produce for self consumption. It is important to give benevolent offerings to the people and keep forever a heart of love for the people."

The people of Shang believed in heavenly-preordained destiny, yet they held that the transfer of preordained fate was caused by the corruption of virtue. Therefore, in commemoration of his father, Zu Yi said, "When heaven endows people with different lengths of life, it does not intentionally do so. But it is because people shortened their lives halfway. Some people can not keep to virtuous actions and refuse punishment from the gods. When heaven gives orders to correct their behavior, they refute this by saying, 'What can heaven do to me?'" Zuo Yi went on, "Our forefathers set examples for us with their fine

Pan Geng, king of the Shang Dynasty, moved the capital to the city Yin, establishing the first stable capital in Chinese history. The picture shows a cow's shoulder blade inside with *jiagu* characters excavated from the site of Yin.

virtue, but some of us are intoxicated by wine and women so that they have discarded the fine virtues of our forefathers." He believed that in everyday life, "heaven can listen and see because the people are listening and seeing; heaven can reward and punish because it is the people who do so. This is because heaven and the people are communicating." So, the political life of a dynasty is preordained by heaven, the length of the political life is closely linked with the virtues of the ruling group.

Collection of Ancient Texts deals with nine realms of ruling a state, the sixth of which includes three virtues in running a society, namely: honesty, hardness, and softness. Being calm, sound, and upright is within honesty; being strong and powerful is among hardness; and being smooth and easy-going with compromises is within the category of softness.

Lord Zhou Gong told Kang Shu, "When you are administering the land inhabited by the people of the fallen Yin Dynasty, it is important to visit the aged and mature men to learn about the causes for the failure of the Yin Dynasty. You should know that the rise of the Zhou Dynasty was because King Wen showed his benevolence and virtue, and he treated the people carefully and never dared to bully the weak and the widows. That is why he received the support of heaven. People will only yield to words of virtue. You should not indulge yourself with wine, and you should also not let your subordinates do so. You should remember that King Wen warned his ministers that wine was served in commemorating ceremonies. A king should keep good virtue instead of indulging in wine. You should understand that the kings of the early Yin Dynasty were enlightened and virtuous as well. You should keep heavenly virtues in mind, never forget that you were born into the family of the king, and you should shoulder important political responsibilities."

As is recorded, when Regent Zhou Gong was preparing to return the throne to Prince Cheng, he repeatedly advised the Prince, "We have to draw a lesson from the Xia Dynasty and the Yin Dynasty. I dare not say that I know the Xia Dynasty was preordained for longer rule and how long that should have been. It was because they ignored virtue that they lost favor before their time. I dare not say that I know that the Yin Dynasty should have lasted longer, but failed to do so also because they failed to esteem virtue. So they lost the fortunate fate given to them by heaven. Now that Your Majesty have accepted the celestial ordinance, we must draw a lesson from them and carry forward their successful experiences. We have just taken up the throne and we live in a new city, so we must immediately consider virtue effectively. If you can keep doing so, you will have a long and lasting rule."

Recorded in another chapter, Pu Hou, the chief justice, gave the following advice to King Mu of the Zhou Dynasty, "Only virtuous might is worthy of respect and fear, and only virtuous radiance is the brightest. An intelligent ruler should educate people to respect fine virtues. The solemn and esteemed one sits above as the king and the honest and sharp ones serve as ministers. Their good virtues shine and all the people will work hard to maintain the virtues. Thus, justice will remain impartial and we will lead the people in a stable social environment to observe the esteemed principles of ethics." Finally, the chief justice summed up by saying, "Only by shouldering heavenly virtue and implementing your own benevolent mission can you enjoy the heavenly rewards of mankind." So, in the cultural tradition of the Zhou Dynasty, ministers attached importance to the function of the criminal code, but they attached greater importance to the fine virtues of those in power that were running society. The criminal code was only a complementary means to the virtuous rule.

(3) Kingly Way and Social Justice

After taking political power in 1100 B.C., King Wu of the Zhou Dynasty visited Qi Zi in the hope of learning more about the theory of harmonious co-existence and orderly ethics. Qi Zi, as an old minister of the previous Shang Dynasty, put forth valuable political ideas on benevolent governance. The idea of governance with virtue emphasized that the ruling group might obtain heavenly support to preserve the political life of the dynasty through fine virtues. The concept of benevolent governance further demanded that the ruler maintain a fair and just political life instead of managing society according to his own subjective likes or dislikes. The so-called "benevolent governance" meant a fair and just social and political order. The goal of refraining from being partial, avoiding favoritism, and not forming parties became the ideological source for an ideal society that later Confucian scholars and ancient Chinese philosophers pursued.

In the late years of the Spring and Autumn Period, Lao Zi (c. 571-471 B.C.), the founder of Taoism, developed the ideology of benevolent governance of the Zhou Dynasty that had been learned from the people of the previous Yin Dynasty, and he developed the political ideology of cherishing virtue and following Taoism. After that, Confucian ideologists such as Confucius, Mencius, and Xun Zi gradually developed the political ideology of "benevolent governance" during the next 500 years. The Confucian scholars gradually dominated the ruling ideology after the years of Emperor Wu of the Han Dynasty, and the political ideal of benevolent governance evolved into the highest form of the political ideal of the Confucian school. During the pre-Qin Dynasty period, Confucian thinkers developed the concept of benevolent governance into the social ideal of common harmony and put forward the ideal of great benevolent governance and service to the public. The dialogue between Confucius and his disciple Zi You expressed their wish for a common harmonious society.

One day, after attending a service ceremony to a hundred gods in the State of Lu, Confucius felt extremely sad about the inadequacy of the ceremony, and so he went up to the tower and produced a loud sigh. You Zi, his disciple, asked him, "Master, why did you sigh?" Confucius answered, "I failed to live in the best times of the Xia, Shang, and Zhou dynasties when elites were in power, so I could only read about this. When benevolent rule was the order of the day, all the people enjoyed public services. Those with virtues and capabilities were elected to run matters, and there was trust, love and friendship. So people respected their parents and loved their children as they did all other people. The aged could live a long life in happiness; the middle-aged could bring into play their talents and capabilities; children could develop in good health; the widows, the sick, and the disabled were cared for; men had jobs and women had their marriages. People feared that materials might be discarded as waste before they had had their full use, but they did not necessarily take them back to their own homes. The fact that people feared that their talents and capability could not be put to good use was not necessarily because of their personal interests. Therefore, there were no sinful and criminal intentions and there was neither theft nor robbery. People shut their doors to prevent the wind and cold rather than the thieves. They did not have to lock the doors tight. Such a society was a harmonious society."

The aforementioned common, harmonious society was indeed an ideal society of Great Harmony, and it was a blueprint for a harmonious society designed by the Confucian scholars of the pre-Qin Dynasty period through a summing up of the ideals of the ancient society of benevolent governance. Later Kang Youwei recorded new forms of expression in his book entitled *The Great Commonwealth* (《大同书》). It described a society in which mankind got rid of the boundaries of nations, classes, races, men and women, families, and industries, everything except the differentiation between men and animals. In a word, "The road to Great Harmony means supreme peace, fairness, benevolence, and ruling with these."

3. "To Keep Intact for Supreme Harmony, Under Which Interest will Be Virtuous"

The Changes of Zhou (《周易》) is a book used to predict the future by the ancient Chinese. It may be called a classic work on decision-making. Due to the limitations of the ancient people's understanding of nature, the book contains many mystical aspects. *Selected Works on Changes* (《易传》) deals with philosophical explanations of *The Book of Changes* (《易经》) by outstanding scholars from the late Spring and Autumn Period to the mid-Warring States Period. Only ten important essays were selected from many philosophical dissertations to be included in that work. *The Book of Changes* and *Selected Works on Changes* have become known as *The Changes of Zhou*.

In general, people attached great importance to the profound philosophical theories in *The Changes of Zhou*, particularly the

A painting of Eight Trigrams in *The Changes of Zhou*

philosophical wisdom that everything is in a state of change and that the rule is to make no changes in the changes. This understanding had nothing wrong in it. However, it covered the political ideology of valuing harmony with habitual modes of thinking. As a matter of fact, *The Changes of Zhou* contains rich and splendid thoughts on valuing harmony. A philosophical theme in the *Selected Works on Changes* is that all the benefits acquired by mankind would be just, effective, and lasting only through creating a harmonious and peaceful social and political environment. The essay entitled "Significance of Changes" from the *Selected Works on Changes* has explicit instructions. It says, "Heaven and the earth interact; *Yin* and *Yang* interflow; softness and hardness interchange. This forms the substance of everything. Everything hopes to grow and dislikes death. People who were fond of and had a profound understanding of all kinds of changes wrote the book of "Changes", which embodied the wisdom of the highest form of harmony."

The current world is in a time of economic globalization and cultural globalization. Nevertheless, the shadow of nuclear war is not completely out of the picture. How to develop a mode of economic development under the theory of social peace poses ideological challenges to the philosophy of human existence and development. I believe that the Chinese traditional philosophy of valuing harmony may result in new philosophical thinking, which should include the following four aspects.

First, all countries in the world need to develop the world economy through peaceful economic exchanges and to obtain their own national interest in the process of the development of economic globalization.

Second, it is important to have an optimal mode of economic development with harmony between man and nature, which includes ecological harmony and environmental safety.

Third, it is essential to attach importance to harmony between individuals and the society. The development of a social economy should have the goal of promoting happiness for the people rather than the growth of profits.

Fourth, it is the harmony of the mental and physical conditions of humankind. At a time of upgrading material life, man should have harmony in his own body and mind to avoid huge psychological fluctuations, especially avoiding the mode of economic development that may cause raptures between body and mind.

(1) "To Keep Intact for Supreme Harmony, Under Which Interest will Be Virtuous"

Of many a philosophical explanations in the *Selected Works on Changes*, the political philosophy expressed in "On Judgment" deserves special attention. It puts forth the brilliant thinking of keeping intact for supreme harmony, under which interest will be virtuous. To keep intact for supreme harmony means that people need to make subjective efforts to keep a continuing peaceful social environment. Only when a society is in a continuing peaceful and harmonious situation, can a man's actions to gain profit, merits will be morally just, and the social profits and achievements will genuinely belong to him. The supreme harmony envisioned here is not a naturally harmonious situation but is one created under the guidance of thinking of the pursuit after peace. It embodies human awareness in taking action to pursue peace and harmony.

Many scholars throughout history have given different explanations of this philosophy. Zhu Xi (1130-1200), a great philosopher of the Southern Song Dynasty (1127-1279), explained it as guaranteeing coordination for supreme harmony: from the aspects of both natural philosophy and social philosophy. He believed that the supreme harmony refers to the peaceful harmony that emerges after a mingling of *Yin* and *Yang*. Keeping intact refers to the perfect situation after anything gains its life. This was used as the fundamental spirit to explain virtuous interest.

In his *Commentaries on the Changes of Zhou* (《周易外传》), Wang Fuzhi (1619-1692), a great philosopher of the Qing Dynasty (1644-1911), gave his explanation with emphasis on human endeavors by placing more stress on the positive role of "keeping intact" over "supreme harmony." Harmony is created through human effort and coordination. Without the effort and coordination, the heterogeneous mass of nature will worm its way in. And there will be surplus or insufficiency. So there must be human efforts to get rid of the surplus and make up for the insufficiency. The rites to standardize human life were implemented and therefore, an ideal society of harmony was developed. In Wang Fuzhi's mind, fame, merits, position, and interest were the results of the natural evolution of virtue of supreme harmony. Wang Fuzhi said, "Social achievements and profits are the inevitable social results of a supreme harmonious environment, and the social position of everyone is the result of the social choice that the supreme harmony of social environment inevitably led to."

In his book *Supplementary Commentaries on the Changes of Zhou* (《周易内传》), Wang Fuzhi further stressed that *qiangua* (male divinity) entirely relied on his pure hard strength and reproductive virtue to lead to the growth and changes of all living creatures and to let them run their own due course. Therefore, the changes of all things followed the right rule of *qiangua* and their own internal regular rule to develop and grow without personal impediments or personal injuries. On the contrary, the strong and the weak might protect each other and seek cooperation so as to coordinate in line with the supreme harmony. This was the profound truth that the right rule generates benefits through which everyone gains. Obviously Wang Fuzhi, based on the changes in nature, illustrated the harmonious relations between social justice and social achievement and progress. A just social environment would bring about benefits for mankind while everyone should gain their benefits in a fair way embodied by social justice.

In the mind of Wang Fuzhi, intelligent rulers should learn from the saints because they were able to follow the rule of nature and let everything develop in due course so that they could co-exist in harmony and prosperity. As Wang Fuzhi put it, "A saint who started from honesty and moved to enlightened virtue was able to envision and discern the situation for the development of matter. As soon as a thing came into being until its end, there would be no mistakes but rather appropriate modifications from infancy to old age. Everything is changing and developing with its proper progress. Everything is making its progress without knowing it and developing and growing along with its nature. What the saint did was just like the operation of the natural wheel of supreme harmony to let everything gain its just benefit."

One may see that the ancient Chinese philosophers were inclined to put their emphasis on examples of changes in nature in order to illustrate the actions of mankind in pursuit of the interests when they were explaining "keeping intact for supreme harmony." Very few of them had the following understanding: Political actions were taken to create a harmonious social environment in order to ensure justice and sustainability in the pursuit of benefits. Wang Fuzhi, living in the turmoil years of the late Ming Dynasty and early Qing Dynasty, witnessed the sufferings brought about by political chaos, and so he had a more profound philosophical view in elaborating the philosophical theme of "changes." He attached greater importance to mankind's conscientious actions in keeping coordination for supreme harmony. The thinking of Wang Fuzhi has positive significance in our current understanding of world peace as being more important than economic and social development in the time of globalization. It is also enlightening. When every member of human society finds his due position and role in the society, that society will have a genuine situation of harmony and all the interests of society will be just and sustainable.

The authors of the *Selected Works on Changes* often gave eulogies to the rulers of their ideal by way of extolling heaven. Heaven, as the leader of all substances in the universe, operates in a selfless and harmonious way, and all the states will thus have tranquility. The authors praised heaven for its selfless and fair virtue in bringing suitability to the creation of all substances. "Man and the beginning" is the starting point of everything and "interests" and "virtues" are the essence and substance of heaven. Heaven, from the very beginning, brought about great concern for everything without saying that it was the result of its granting favors. "Oh, great heaven, you are almighty and powerful, neutral and excellent, and pure."

(2) "What Unites People? Wealth Is the Answer"

In *The Changes of Zhou*, the author discusses two key issues: How to keep one's position, and how to unite people. His answer was: to unite people with wealth; to keep one's position through virtue and benevolence. Thus the political philosophical ideology of *The Changes of Zhou* has the distinctive classic feature of putting people first. The goal of the development of social economy should be directed toward the unity of people rather than the pursuit of pure self interest. Wealth and goods are things that everybody likes, but people should not do things at the cost of morals and virtues. Any wealth and goods gained through immoral means will be lost in the final analysis. This shows that the legitimacy for all economic activities should first be based on morals so as to ensure sustainability.

The contention for resources of development among nations and countries was the main cause of the two world wars in the first half of the 20th century. The emergence of nuclear weapons has changed the nature of war for mankind. Nuclear deterrence in the post cold-war period reduced greatly the possibility of a world war. However, the process of contending for resources in technology as the front-runner and talented people close behind is accelerating. The knowledge economy and information economy of post-industrial society is intensifying the contention. Therefore, the matter of which of the two, economic development or humanitarianism, is now the goal that determines different modes of economic development.

What unites people? The answer is "wealth." A first look will find that wealth is quite important and people cannot be united without wealth. However, a deeper analysis shows that wealth is used for uniting people. Therefore, uniting people is the purpose for which wealth should be used, and wealth should be only an instrument for uniting people. When we lack wealth, we need to create a huge volume of wealth in order to unite people. However, we should keep in mind that wealth is only a means and should not be treated as the goal. The ultimate value of wealth is embodied in uniting people. So the traditional Confucian debate over "rights and interests" demanded that the ruling group put justice as the social principle over the goal of acquiring of wealth. Just as the *Great Learning* (《大学》) put it, the ruler will have the people only when he has fine virtues; he will have territories only when he has the people; he will have wealth only when he has territories; he will put social functions into place when he has wealth. Fine political virtue is the fundamental for ruling society and wealth is only secondary. If the cart is put before the horse, the people will contend among themselves. When the rulers collect all the wealth, the people will be disunited. When the wealth of the rulers is distributed to society, people will become united. So administrative orders given in an improper way will have a feedback of social smears, and wealth acquired in unfair ways will be consumed by unreasonable approaches.

Of course, we may criticize traditional Confucian school for maintaining a principle of social justice that was in question because the justice was preconditioned on the system of classes. However, the concept of demanding that the rulers and the state put social justice as the priority and particularly demand that officials not contend for wealth against the common people is entirely correct.

The philosophy of changes emphasized that man should be superseded in the process of economic development as opposed to directly taking interest as the goal of economic activities. Therefore, the tradition particularly stressed that the goal of economic activity should be rational, and it defined the significance of economic activity as a force uniting society rather than being directed toward profits. This thinking found similar expressions in Lao Zi, the founder of Taoism. Lao Zi said, "Between fame and life, which is closer to man? Between life and goods, which deserves more attention? Of gains and losses, which causes more harm? So, the more care, the higher the cost will be. The more that is stored, the more the losses will be. To know satisfaction will not lead to humiliation. To know where to stop will not find danger, and the state political power will last for a long time." He also reproached the then ruler by saying, "The people are hungry because rulers collect too many taxes. The people are difficult to be ruled over because the rulers are too nit-picking. The people disparage death because the rulers cherish their lives too much.... The court is spick and span and the field is desolate and the storage place is empty. The rulers are in decent clothes, wearing swords, and buried under wine and women with sufficient wealth and materials. This is a frivolous social phenomenon instead of one of morals."

As far as one's personal life is concerned, the philosophy of changes also put forth the idea that in life the all-round development of personality should be taken as the goal.

As far as the pursuit of interest and the development of personality is concerned, the authors of the *Selected Works on Changes* were opposed to the practice of some people seeking after wealth at the risk of their own lives, but demanded that they realize that the main purpose for the pursuit after interest was for the safety of their own lives and thereafter the upgrading of their virtues. The authors of the *Selected Works on Changes* disparaged those who pursued economic interests shamefully as lesser men. They quoted Confucius' criticism, "Lesser men do not feel shameful of being immoral, do not respectfully fear unjust actions, do not make any efforts to achieve anything if there is no interest, and refuse to be on guard if there is no threat." Later Confucian thinkers put this in a more concise way, calling the action "making a fortune at the risk of one's life." In the book the *Great Learning*, a classic of the pre-Qin Dynasty period, opposition to "making fortune at the risk one's life" was particularly stressed and people were encouraged "to improve life with wealth," to have all-round development, and to meet the diversified needs of a life with wealth.

How to unite people had its historical connotation as well as a principle of far-reaching significance. Historically, this principle encouraged the uniting of many people so that a country could develop its economy. This was a requirement for social development at a time when the land was vast and the population small.

In today's society, the traditional theme of "uniting people" may evolve into the more profound philosophical view of putting people first. The significance of this ancient philosophical theme lies not only in the question of amassing talents but also in the matter of how to mobilize the will of the people of the whole society in order to lead them toward an ideal system and society.

(3) Dialectical Relationship Between a Harmonious Social Environment and the Justice and Sustainability of Economic Development

Today when economic strength and military force are in the dominant position, peace in the international community often becomes just a moral slogan. As mankind entered the 1960s, along with the post-industrial society, the destruction of the global ecology, and intensification of regional conflicts, human beings were forced to rethink the question of the mode of economic development. Especially because of the intensified destruction of the environment by developing countries, people were urged to ponder the issue of justice and the sustainability of economic development. In presenting the problems, we may draw strength from the wisdom of ancient times. The philosophy of "keeping intact for supreme harmony under which interest shall be virtuous" in the *Selected Works on Changes* has already given us the clue: Creating a harmonious and peaceful social environment is the prerequisite to justice and the sustainability of economic development. Without a harmonious and peaceful social environment, the justice of economic activities and the potential of sustained development will certainly be questionable.

The Chinese traditional agricultural society attached importance to harmony between man and nature, mainly stressing that men should let nature develop along its own course and they should do their farming according to the seasons. The economic development of modern society has more to follow besides this basic natural rule. It has to meet the internal needs of human beings, so economic development must be united to social harmony. Only by doing thus, will the economic development be just and the potential of development sustainable.

The matter of "keeping intact for supreme harmony under which interest will be virtuous" later evolved into a matter of "interest vs. rights, or benevolent rule vs. tyrannical rule." The issue of justice and sustainability of a harmonious society and economic development evolved into ethical issues related to interests or rights, and into philosophical issues related to benevolent rule or tyrannical rule. In other words, they became issues of economic and political ethics. This was the result of deepening of understanding. "Issues of interests or rights" were debated as economic ethical problems to determine if economic activities were in line with moral requirements. The traditional Chinese, particularly the Confucian thinkers, attached great importance to ethical modes in the pursuit of interests by businessmen and objected to any unethical profiteering activities. The issue of benevolent rule or tyrannical rule was discussed as a means of legitimacy of political rule. A ruler with strong political powers was tyrannical if he used violent methods to rule the people or handle relations with other peoples. A ruler would be a benevolent ruler if he won trust and support of the people through benevolent ways and if other peoples were willing to maintain a peaceful co-inhabitance with him. One of the contents of benevolent rule was that everybody under heaven should have his concern. As the *Xi Message* (《系辞》) put it, Shennong took the power to rule after Baoxi and taught people to cut down trees in order to make farming tools. At noontime, people came to the fair to trade. Everybody got what he needed. So, benevolent governance in the ancient Chinese political ideal was the politics of harmony, benevolence, and freedom for the people. Just as Mencius said when he was advising Duke Xuan of Qi, "Now if Your Excellency can reform politics and implement benevolence, all the educated people will want to be officials of the State of Qi; all the farmers will want to farm in the State of Qi; all the businessmen will want to do business in the State of Qi; all the travelers will want to travel to and through the State of Qi, and all those who hate their dukes or kings will want to come to complain to the State of Qi. If you can achieve this, who will be able to resist you?"

As a matter of fact, there were other phrases for valuing harmony in *The Changes of Zhou*. A typical one was *taigua* whose divinatory symbol was a female on top of a male, symbolizing that the strong humbly lay under the weaker to form a peaceful and tranquil situation. *The Changes of Zhou* explained the symbol as, "The *Yin* and *Yang* copulate under heaven; everything grows smoothly; the emperor and ministers work in a concerted effort; and the whole society has a common ideal. Therefore, in this situation, the behaviors of gentlemen increasingly develop while the behaviors of lesser men decline. A harmonious social situation will come, and it will last long." Zhang Zai, a Confucian scholar of the later Song Dynasty, went further, "Harmony and happiness are indeed the beginning of the great right way. Harmony will be broader and happiness will last. The nature of the movement of heaven and earth is lasting and broad."

Chapter II

Zheng He's Oceanic Voyages and China's Foreign Policy of Peace

The "benevolent governance" of the Confucian school and the "governance with virtue" of the Taoist school had a profound impact on the thinking of politicians in Chinese traditional society. In handling the relations of the Han people with other ethnic groups, they often used the method of moral incitement rather than military threats. The thinking of luring those who did not yield through benevolent politics and with the method of rectifying rites and music put forward by Confucius was the ideological principle used in the handling of relations among dukes, and the brilliant idea of ruling with virtue was often used by later politicians in handling relations with the nationalities at the borders. Even today, the thinking has some important enlightening significance. If a far away nation or country does not want to yield to a big power, the leader of the power makes efforts in the construction of the cultural system and social order instead of resorting to military force to threaten others, and making his country a wonderland for others who admire his people's living standards, and then those countries and their peoples will voluntarily accept his cultural and political model. Under the influence of "governance with virtue," the ancient Chinese politicians developed the special system of "*jimi*," namely, a method for cultivating the good will of the people of minority ethnic groups at the borders and keeping contact with them so that they would not be disloyal. The word of "*jimi*" was first formally used by the historian Sima Qian in the *Records of the Historian* (《史记》) in 2nd century B.C. "*Jimi*" was a tactic, and today people regard it as having produced the obvious superiority of the Han culture. Historically, it was a peaceful diplomatic policy. This tactic gradually developed into a system over a long time of political rule, which mainly included measures such as the sending of envoys, conferring titles, establishing vassal states, sending princess to marry the leader of a state, mutual trade, and taking an oath of alliance.

Under the influence of "governance with virtue," ancient politicians in China endeavored to address relations with the various nationalities on the borders through peaceful means, and they seldom took the approach of war in contending for resources needed for social development. They had a profound understanding of Lao Zi's thinking that "weapons are ill-omened things." Emperor Wu (156-87 B.C.) of the Han Dynasty sent troops up north to fight the Huns because he thought he had no other way. In later years, he reconsidered his frequent use of military forces and warned his successors not to follow his example. Emperor Xuan (62-49 B.C.) of the Han Dynasty made an announcement of self-incrimination, saying that the people at the borders failed to yield to him because his virtues were not up to it yet, so he would change his policy toward the border regions into one of peace and tranquility at the border. Thus, one may see that the Chinese, under the influence of a cultural tradition of governance with virtue, greatly cherished peaceful means in handling relations with the nationalities on their borders.

The Chinese people have never neglected interaction and exchanges with ethnic groups at the border, but have attached importance to internal social development as regards the question of economic development. On the vast land of China, the internal society had a great potential for development. The fact that Zheng He (1371-1433) of the early Ming Dynasty made seven oceanic voyages long before the arrival of the modern world is a typical example of the fact that Chinese society took the road of self-development with peaceful foreign relations, such as the sending of envoys and starting trade. This peaceful foreign line was consistent with the fundamental spirit of diplomacy in sending envoys, arranging marriages, and doing trade business in Chinese history.

1. Zheng He's Seven Oceanic Voyages

Zheng He's voyages were world-shaking events in the history of oceanic travel before the coming of the modern world. They showed that humankind had upgraded its capabilities in overcoming obstacles and making use of the ocean. Today, different people may have different assessments of the significance of Zheng He's voyages. As far as trade was concerned, they did not have much significance because the high techniques of his voyages failed to turn into any commercial value and so did not promote a breakthrough in the development of world economy and trade. On the contrary, his seven voyages were all taken on the orders of the emperor at great cost so as to spread the emperor's prestige. There was no intent to promote the economic development of China. However, from the point of view of political, diplomatic, and cultural exchanges, his seven voyages had enlightening significance and he set an example in pioneering peaceful diplomacy and cultural exchanges.

Zhu Di (1360-1424), Emperor Chengzu of the Ming Dynasty, was a tyrannical emperor who made some achievements. As far as the political struggle for power was concerned, he was indeed ruthless. He was as ambitious as his father, Zhu Yuanzhang (1328-1398), the founder of the Ming Dynasty. Emperor Chengzu had many motives in sending out Zheng He on the oceanic voyages and the personal motivation of the emperor was a secret never to be released. But from the historical results, one may see the seven oceanic voyages over 28 years had a greater positive role on history than just the initial political motivations of the emperor. First, the seven voyages were mainly for peaceful cultural exchanges without any military action toward conquering the countries Zheng He visited. They were all peaceful exchanges with other countries. Second, through the seven voyages, China established friendly interactive relations with the various south Pacific, south Asian, and even African countries such as Somalia. They enhanced understanding and promoted cultural exchanges between nations. Third, they played a role in enlightening the Chinese people about knowledge of the world.

The significance of these historical events to later generations was often influenced by the practical needs of the people of later generations. As an Italian philosopher once said, "Any history is the history of contemporary times." As for the economic globalization and multi-culturalism of today, we may draw political and diplomatic wisdom from the seven voyages made by Zheng He. The foreign policy of peace and cultural exchanges for peace will benefit China as well as other countries. Even as China's economy is developing with the possession of many advanced technologies, China will stick to cultural and economic exchanges in a peaceful way in its contacts with other countries. This will win the friendship of peoples from other countries.

(1) Zheng He's Voyages and the Promotion and Development of Chinese Civilization to the Cultures of the East Asian Nations

According to historical records, from 1405 to 1433, Zheng He made seven oceanic voyages. During the seven trips, he loyally carried out the peaceful foreign policy of the Ming Dynasty in "making friends rather than profits" and "more going than coming." He and his crew were welcomed by the local governments and people wherever they went. Only on a few occasions did they have small and temporary skirmishes with local governments, and finally they turned all swords into ploughshares.

On the 11th of July in 1405, Zheng He, at the instruction of Emperor Yongle, started his voyage to countries of the south Pacific. At that time, the fleet consisted of 62 "treasure ships" with 27,800 people, including officials and crewmen. The grand fleet started from Liujiagang Port and progressed down the Yangtze River to the East China Sea, then to the Changle Port in Fujian Province, where they conducted a prayer ceremony, and then moved on into the Pacific. Zheng He and his party took with them gold coins. At each place they docked, they read the emperor's proclamation of harmonious co-existence and gave the valuable gifts to the leaders of the various localities. They visited over a dozen countries on their first voyage, including Champa, Java, Palembang, Sumatra, Malacca, and Aru.

On the second voyage, they made calls on eight countries including Champa, Java, Siam, Sumatra, Nanwuli, Ceylon, Kozhikode, and Cochin.

During the third voyage they visited fourteen countries including Champa, Java, Siam, Sumatra, Ceylon, Cochin, Kozhikode, and Quilon.

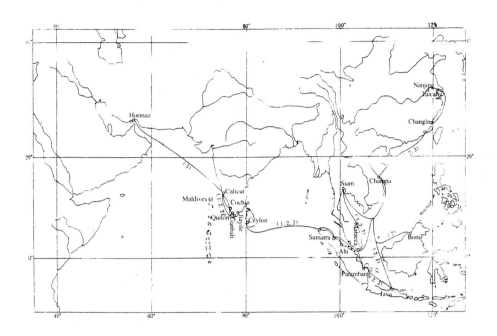

A sketch map illustrating the routes followed by Zheng He on his first three voyages

During their fourth voyage, they stopped at various south Asian countries such as Palembang and Java, and they went as far as to Hormuz in the Persian Gulf of the Arabian Sea. A branch of the fleet was sent to the Maldives, and it reached Mogadishu and Brawa in Somalia, East Africa and Kenya. Then it returned to Hormuz.

The fifth voyage was mainly conducted to return envoys from countries such as Palembang and Java.

The sixth voyage was to return envoys from countries around Hormuz.

Six of the seven voyages took place under the reign of Emperor Chengzu of the Ming Dynasty. When the ships returned from the first voyage in 1407, envoys from countries such as Java, Sumatra, and Kozhekode joined Zheng He's fleet in order to visit China. After the third voyage, envoys from countries such as Kozhekode, Cochin, and Sumatra visited the Ming Dynasty. After the fourth voyage, envoys from African countries such as Mogadishu went along with the fleet to visit the Ming Dynasty. The fifth and sixth voyages were mainly to return those envoys. This demonstrated the courtesy and hospitality of the Ming Dynasty as much as it did the spirit of a foreign policy of peace.

In 1433, eight years after Emperor Xuanzong succeeded Emperor Chengzu, Zheng He and Jinghong made another voyage so as to intensify the ties with overseas countries. The psychology of Emperor Xuanzong was quite interesting. As the emperor of the Ming Dynasty, he was much interested in the matter of foreign envoys. This shows, to a certain extent, that the Chinese people had begun to have a hazy awareness of the world. Though their view was still that China during the Ming Dynasty was a big country and needed envoys from other countries to make courtesy calls, the Dynasty greatly feared isolation. As the emperor of the

A painting of a *fulu* (zebra from Africa) from the Ming Dynasty *Pictures of Exotic Things* (*Yiwu Tuzhi*)

Ming Dynasty, he could get nowhere without relations with the outside world. From these personal concerns of Emperor Xuanzong, one can see that the successful foreign policy of his two ambitious predecessors had linked China with the world. So Emperor Xuanzong found that the emperor of the Ming Dynasty felt lonely and isolated without the world.

Naturally, during the long process of a voyage, and due to occasional political reasons or the influence of some emergency events, Zheng He's fleet did engage in armed conflicts with some local forces. However, under the guiding principle of peaceful diplomacy and cultural exchanges, these skirmishes were rapidly resolved. Zheng He's fleet arrived at Ceylon during the second voyage in 1408. The state religion there was Buddhism, but the then king of Ceylon did not respect Buddhist rules and was quite cruel, inflicting great suffering on the people. Seeing that Zheng He and his entourage had brought with them a large number of gold and silver wares and other treasures, the king sent his son to lure Zheng He and the entourage from the Treasure Ship and then catch them in a blackmailing plot so that he could obtain the treasure. Zheng He saw through this plot and made use of the situation of the city being empty of troops because the king sent his men out. Zheng He led his train to attack and take over the city, and he captured the king and his wife as well as his officials. Zheng He then took them back to the emperor of the Ming Dynasty. Nevertheless, Emperor Chengzu took an extremely lenient attitude. Instead of killing them, he ordered the people to send them back. From then on, China and Ceylon returned to the good relations they had had in the past and continued to send envoys to each other's countries and to keep friendly relations for over two centuries.

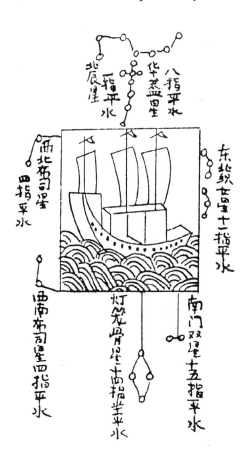

A stellar measuring chart for the return voyage from Ceylon to Sumatra

As an envoy of peace, Zheng He, on his voyage into the western ocean, used armed forces to defeat pirates. On his voyage, he caught the chieftain of a tribe in Palembang, which was an ancient country established in the 7th century on the island of Sumatra. Chieftain Chen and his men were capturing and robbing merchant ships on the seas of southeastern Asia. Zheng He sent him a memorandum demanding that this practice stop. Chen pretended to surrender but instead stole the goods and materials of Zheng He's fleet. Zheng He then led his men to fight the pirate and captured him. So peace on the route of merchant ships of the south Pacific was maintained.

Zheng He served under the rein of Emperor Chengzu, Emperor Renzong and Emperor Xuanzong of the Ming Dynasty for 28 years, in which he made seven oceanic voyages to the west going through more than 30 countries and regions. After Zheng He visited these places, one envoy after another was sent to the Ming Dynast to strengthen the political and economic relations with the Ming Dynasty, which escorted them back to their home countries. Along the navigation routes, some merchants conducted economic and trade business. Through these economic activities, cultural exchanges with these different nations were promoted and intensified. Thus the Chinese "Silk Road" on the sea was particularly flourishing.

(2) The Awareness of the World and the Cultural Concept of Reaching out to the World of the Chinese in the 15th Century

The Chinese society after the Qin (221-206 B.C.) and Han (206 B.C.-A.D. 220) dynasties witnessed ambitious emperors who had their own awareness of the world, except some mean emperors during split periods. Traditional China was not a closed inland country. Though traditionally China showed the feature of an inland country and did not have sufficient under-standing, exploration and utilization of the value of the ocean, it does not mean that traditional Chinese did not have the desire to have contact with peoples of other countries in the world. On the contrary, the traditional China with long land borders learned to have peaceful co-existence with different peoples at the borders, which was one of its major political and diplomatic goals. After establishing the Ming Dynasty in 1368, Emperor Zhu Yuanzhang immediately took an active diplomatic policy to develop relations with na-tionalities at the borders. According to studies of experts on the Ming Dy-nasty, in the year of establishment of the Ming Dynasty, Emperor Zhu Yuanzhang sent envoys with credentials to Korea and northern Viet Nam. In the following year, he sent envoys to Japan, southern Viet Nam, Java of In-donesia and other countries. In 1370, he sent envoys to Thailand, southern Sumatra, northern Kalimantan and Cambodia. In 1395, the Emperor sent envoys out across the border in all directions. These envoys visited nation-alities at the border and 36 countries across the border and learned about 31 different countries. Eighteen bigger countries and 49 smaller ones had strik-ingly different customs from that of China. Besides, some oceanic countries had exchanges with China, including envoys and businessmen. Historical facts showed that from the 14th century, the Chinese people had a quite clear awareness of the world, however, the world in their mind was not as wide as it is now. Emperor Zhu Yuanzhang had an explicit foreign policy by saying "Do not resort to the use of force easily even if there are some misunderstandings or conflicts in the process of exchanges so long as those countries do not pose a threat to the Ming Dynasty." This fully exemplified the diplomatic thinking of peace by Emperor Zhu Yuanzhang. His political purpose of sending out envoys to countries at the borders was mainly to keep good relations with nations at the border and maintain peace and tranquility at the border.

After succeeding his father's throne, Emperor Chengzu enthusiastically followed the laid-down foreign policy and doubled the efforts to smooth the political relations with neighboring countries by sending out capable eunuchs as envoys to further develop international relations. In respect of foreign policy, Emperor Chengzu set forth strong political principles for Zheng He's oceanic voyage, such as "preaching benevolence while being gentle with foreigners," "more going than coming." Therefore, as far as foreign policy was concerned, Emperor Chengzu stressed more on "governance with virtue" and prestige, whose aim was political rather than economic.

According to the record of *History of the Ming Dynasty* (《明史》), under the rein of Emperor Chengzu, it was mostly senior eunuchs of the court who were given the task and endeavored to develop passages to and relations with the peoples at the border. They made special contributions to peace diplomacy and cultural exchanges. Among them, Zheng He and Jing Hong as envoys made oceanic voyages in the west, Li Da went to western inland countries, Hai Tong went northbound while Hou Xian went westbound to today's Qinghai and Tibet and sometimes as far as to east India.

In 1415, Hou Xian arrived in Bangladesh. The king of Bangladesh sent his envoy to the Ming Dynasty and presented gift of giraffe to Emperor Chengzu, who was very much pleased and reciprocated with better present. To the west of Bangladesh and in the middle of India, there was a kingdom of Janapur, which was one of the ancient countries that believed in Buddhism. It intended to invade Bangladesh. The king of Bangladesh told this to Emperor Chengzu, who sent Hou Xian to mediate the matter in 1420. When Hou Xian arrived in Janapur and presented gold coins and expressed the wishes of the Ming Dynasty of a peaceful settlement, Janapur gave up its intension of invasion. This showed that the Ming Dynasty played a positive role of maintaining peace in dealing with international affairs. In 1427, Hou Xian went to different tribes in Qinghai and Tibet. The *History of the Ming Dynasty* praised highly of Hou Xian for his capability, flexibility and courage. Hou Xian traveled five times to the desolate areas in the west region.

Before Zheng He, Chen Cheng of the Ming Dynasty, another envoy of peace, deserved mentioning. Chen Cheng was the author of *Journey to the West Region* (《西域行程记》) and *Notes of Foreign States in the West Region* (《西域番国志》). Mr. Chen was born in the late Yuan Dynasty and survived four emperors and died approximately in 1457. In 1396, he was first sent to the region somewhere around today's Gansu, Qinghai and Xinjiang. From 1413 to 1415, Chen Cheng made his second trip to the region and together with Li Da to send back envoys with a great deal of presents from Emperor Chengzu of the Ming Dynasty. When Chen Cheng returned, he was given local products like horses as gifts to the Ming emperor. Through his trip to the west, the Ming Dynasty strengthened its relations with peoples in the west region for maintenance of peace.

The aforementioned peaceful diplomatic envoys and cultural messengers show the diplomatic principles of peace maintained by the two ambitious emperors of the early Ming Dynasty. As far as virtues are concerned, the personal motivations of Emperor Chengzu in pioneering the development of relations with bordering countries is not necessarily worthy of praise, but his approaches were peaceful and embodied the cultural concept of the Chinese people in reaching out to the world in a peaceful way. Over one hundred years later, missionaries from the West came to China and the cultural exchanges between China and the West formally began. In the initial period, the cultural exchanges were basically conducted in a peaceful way. Only after the "etiquette dispute" under the reign of Emperor Kangxi (1662-1723) were these peaceful cultural exchanges suspended for a time. In the middle of the reign under Emperor Qianlong (1736-1796), the British envoy George Macartney came to China. Because of the ignorance and arrogance of Emperor Qianlong, the opportunity for peaceful exchanges between the economies and cultures of the two countries were lost. Later, along with the decline of the Qing Dynasty, during the next round of economic and cultural exchanges, China was in a passive position. The reasons for this situation first started with the arrogance of the ruler of the Qing Dynasty. Second was the expansion and invasion of the modern capitalist colonial economy. The rise of capitalist industrialization in the West brought about a higher material civilization to mankind as well as sufferings and humiliations for many countries and nations that would develop afterwards. As humankind entered the 21st century, the recollection of China's peaceful foreign policy in economics, politics, and culture bears recognition in terms of the world's pursuit of peace.

2. Zhang Qian Sent as an Envoy to the Western Regions

Long before Zheng He and his entourage's voyage to the western seas, Zhang Qian (? –114 B.C.), a cultural envoy of peace, was sent twice to countries in the western regions so as to open a Chinese diplomatic road to the west, and he made pioneering contributions to economic and cultural exchanges between China and various countries in the western regions. Sima Qian, the Chinese historian of the Western Han Dynasty (206 B.C.-A.D. 25), praised Zhang Qian's great mission to the western regions as opening up the road to that area.

During the Qin and Han dynasties, the Huns in northern China were a people living on horseback. They were strong and valiant, often invading and disturbing the Han people who were engaged in agriculture as their economic base. How to effectively resist the invasion of the Huns was the constant wish of the Han people during the period of the

A bronze horse unearthed from a Han-dynasty tomb in Gansu. It is said to be an imitation of the Ili horse brought back by Zhang Qian from the western regions.

Qin and Han dynasties. After unifying China, the first emperor of the Qin sent General Meng Tian north in 218 B.C. to drive out the Huns. At the same time he took a passive defensive policy by linking up the old sections of the Great Wall that had first been erected by the states of Qin, Zhao, and Yan. His purpose was to stop invasions of the Huns from the north. After defeating Xiang Yu, Liu Bang, the founding emperor of the Han Dynasty, led a troop, 320,000-strong, into battle at Pingcheng (near today's Datong in Shanxi Province). But he and his troops were encircled by 400,000 Huns, and finally Zhang Liang, his military adviser, bribed the Hun generals to let them escape. Through the efforts of Emperor Wen and Emperor Jing of the Han Dynasty, when it came to the reign of Emperor Wu, the Han Dynasty accumulated material and financial strength so as to provide material provisions for the settlement of the security problem on the northern border. Zhang Qian was then sent as an envoy to the western regions to make alliances with nationalities such as Tukhara so as to achieve joint resistance against the Huns. This was the first event in China's foreign policy of peace.

(1) Zhang Qian Sent as an Envoy to the Western Regions

Zhang Qian came from Hanzhong in Shaanxi Province. Sima Qian praised him as a man of extraordinary tenacity. He was honest and trustworthy, and he was popular among the minority ethnic groups that did not speak the Chinese language. Because Zhang Qian had such a special personality, he was able to return to the Han Dynasty after over a dozen years of hardship and suffering in the places of different nationalities and different countries, even though he could not speak their languages. As the cultural and peaceful envoy of the early Western Han Dynasty, Zhang Qian, at the order of Emperor Wu, went to the western regions (around today's Gansu Province). His original purpose was to forge an alliance with Tukhara in order to resist the Huns. To get Tukhara, Zhang Qian had to pass through the territories of the Huns. When the Huns learned that Zhang Qian was planning to make an alliance with Tukhara, they detained him and said to him: "Tukhara is to the north of us, and you are planning to make contact with them. There must be some political purpose in this. If we Huns want to go through your territory to make contacts with the State of Yue to your south, would you agree?" Thus, Zhang Qian was detained there for more than a dozen years. The Huns asked him to marry a Hun girl and to have children. However, he never forgot his mission and was always reminded of his role as an envoy by the staff given to him by Emperor Wu.

Due to the lack of exchanges between nationalities at that time, the lack of geographic knowledge, and lack of knowledge about the customs of the local people, Zhang Qian's trips to the western regions were extremely difficult. According to the *Records of the Historian*, after Zhang Qian had lived for over a dozen of years in the state of the Huns, they relaxed their surveillance over him. One day, he led his entourage to flee toward the area of Tukhara. Not knowing the road there, the group arrived at Dawan (Ferghana, in the eastern part of Uzbekistan) after walking west for over ten days. The people of Dawan knew that the Han Dynasty was rich and affluent. They had long wanted to have contacts with this Dynasty but had not yet had the opportunity. Now they were more than glad to receive an envoy from the Han Dynasty into their state. They asked about the purpose of Zhang Qian's trip and where he wished to go. He explained his mission to them, and he guaranteed that Dawan would be given many treasures as gifts if they could guide him to the Tukhara. The people of Dawan believed what he said and so they sent a guide to escort the entourage to Tukhara.

Upon arriving at Tukhara, Zhang Qian learned that the king of Tukhara had been killed by the Huns and that the prince had succeeded to the throne and was now subject to the Daxia State. Under the protection of the Daxia and with everything now stable and peaceful, the new king of Tukhara had no desire for revenge against the Huns nor any desire to relate to the Han Dynasty because his state was so far away from the Hans. As Zhang Qian could not have acquired information about the basic political, economic, geographic situation, or customs of Tukhara, he was unable to acquire a clear understanding of the psychology of the Tukhara people. As a result, he returned without the desired achievement. Failing in this political purpose, Zhang Qian had to return to Daxia from Tukhara. After staying there for over a year, he intended to return to the Han Dynasty, but was once more captured by the Huns. Another year passed, and then taking the opportunity of the death of King Chanyu and internal turmoil in the king's family, Zhang Qian fled from the Huns. Only two of the 100-odd people who had traveled with him returned alive after more than 13 years of hardship and suffering.

Though Zhang Qian failed to accomplish his political task, he did bring back many cultural gains. He had recorded what he saw and learned on his way to and from Tukhara and he made a detailed report of this to Emperor Wu. So the Chinese people began to know more about the geography and customs of the western regions.

In 119 B.C., Zhang Qian began his second diplomatic mission to the western regions. The political purpose was to make an alliance with the State of Osun so as to cut off their alliance with the Huns. Due to the long time rule of the Huns, the State of Osun did not immediately agree to an alliance, partly because they were far from the Han Dynasty and did not know how big and how powerful the Han Dynasty was. At that time, the State of Osun also had internal contradictions. The old king had ten sons, and Dalu, the fifth son, was strong but he was not the prince designated to succeed to the throne. The prince to succeed, however, died early and his son, Cenqu, then became the legal successor. The old king, fearing that Dalu might kill Cenqu, provided Cenqu with 10,000 cavalry soldiers, while he kept 10,000 for himself. Shortly thereafter, Dalu led his other brothers in a rebellion and claimed the kingdom for himself. So the State of Osun was thus divided into three parts. Upon his arrival, Zhang Qian did not know this situation at all, and so his lobbying was not successful. When Zhang Qian learned about the matter, he dispatched his deputies to the states of Dawan, Liangju, Tukhara, Daxia, Anxi, and Shendu. The king of Osun sent a guide and translators to escort Zhang Qian on his return to the Han Dynasty. Zhang Qian gave some 10 horses to the guide and translators from Osun. When envoys from Osun later went to the Han Dynasty, they found out how large the Han Dynasty was.

After Zhang Qian returned, Emperor Wu paid great attention to his trip. The pity was that Zhang Qian died the next year. However, the envoys from Osun that followed Zhang Qian to the Han Dynasty reported about the prosperity of the Han Dynasty. The king of Osun began to attach importance to the development of relations with the Han Dynasty. The states that Zhang Qian's deputies went to also sent their envoys to the Han Dynasty. Thus they all learned about the affluence of the Han Dynasty. After that, the Han Dynasty began its political and economic exchanges with the states in the western regions.

Zhang Qian was conferred with the title of Bowang Duke and he used that title during his diplomatic mission to the western regions. Thanks to the noble personality and credibility of Zhang Qian, he won the love and respect from the people of the western regions. After his death, every envoy to the western regions used the title of "Bowang Duke" to demonstrate their guarantee of credibility. The people in the western regions trusted these envoys.

Zhang Qian was the most outstanding Chinese diplomat and cultural adventurer in the second century B.C. He was one of the greatest of the peaceful diplomats in Chinese history. According to the *Records of the Historican*, because Zhang Qian was conferred with the respected title of duke for opening up the road to the western regions, many people thereafter vied in submitting reports to the emperor about their findings of treasures in foreign countries in the hope of catching the eye of and winning support from the emperor so as to acquire an esteemed title. Due to their impure intentions, few were successful. Some even cooked up fake reports that caused the emperor to take military action against the western regions. This sad lesson in the history of diplomacy provides much food for thought regarding today's politicians in various countries.

After Zhang Qian, during the later Han Dynasty there was another peaceful and cultural envoy named Gan Ying. He was given a mission to go to Daqin (Italy of the then Roman Empire), and for the first time set out to pioneer a path from China to Europe. According to the *Book of the Later Han Dynasty*（《后汉书》），in 97, Minister Ban Chao sent Gan Ying as an envoy to Daqin. He first arrived in Tiaozi (the capital of Ancient Syria) and then went on to Daqin. In 166, Emperor Marcus Aurelius Antonius (121-180) sent his envoy to China with ivory, rhinoceros horn, and hawksbill turtle. This was the first contact between the ancient Roman Empire and China.

(2) Monks Went Westward from the 3rd to the 10th Centuries to Seek Buddhist Knowledge and Peaceful Cultural Exchanges Between China and India

Zhang Qian, as an envoy, went twice to the western regions and pioneered the path from China into the states of that area, thus laying a foundation for the economic and cultural exchanges between China and the states of the western regions. Zhang Qian thus played a major part in India's Buddhism coming to China by way of the states of the western regions.

Buddhism began to spread to the states in the western regions around the 3rd century B.C. At the same time that Emperor Wu opened a path to the western regions, Buddhism began to spread eastward. Nevertheless, the Chinese academia of the Eastern Han Dynasty (25-220) worshiped practicality in culture, while the Hinayana Buddhism popular in states in the western regions was mainly concerned with self-salvation. It did not match the spirit of the Confucian school of the Han Dynasty. Therefore, though Buddhism came to China, it did not have much influence on the scholars and officials in China. Early in the 3rd century, because of a cruel political struggle inside the ruling class, some scholars and officials feared for their lives and began to turn from concerns about running the country to concerns about their own fate. It was at this time that some Buddhist ideas began to be acceptable to them. In mid-3rd century, Buddhism grew in popularity in China. Some sincere monks decided to travel westward to find the genuine truth about Indian Buddhism. Zhu Shixing was the first great and outstanding man in Chinese history to go west in search of Buddhist knowledge.

Zhu Shixing reached the western border in the year of 260 and then went further westward to the State of Liyul where he copied 90 chapters of the Sanskrit sutras. The reason he wished to go west to seek Buddhist knowledge was that, after he became a monk, he found something illogical in the teaching of Virtuous Behavior in Buddhism, and so he was determined to go westward to discover the true Buddhism for China. According to the *Book of the Later Han Dynasty*, Yutian was 5,850 kilometers away from Louyang. Zhu Shixing went through the desert, through life and death, for a period of 23 years. He finally arrived at Liyul in 282. He died there but he entrusted others to take the genuine sutras back to China.

From the 3rd to early 5th centuries, it was quite popular for Chinese monks to go west. It was the first peak of cultural exchanges between China and India. During this period, many senior monks, either alone or in groups, went to India to seek Buddhist sutras. Among them there was Kang Falang and three others in the Eastern Jin Dynasty (317-420), and Hui Chang and two others from the late Eastern Jin Dynasty. Also in 404, Zhi Meng and Tan

Chuan with 13 others, and in 420, Fa Yong and 24 others left for India and other countries to seek Buddhist sutras. These two trips resulted in cultural and peaceful exchanges between China and India that lasted for over 100 years. They were thus great events.

During the 100 years or so, Fa Xian (about 337-422), another great traveler to the west, deserves praise. There were increasingly many a kind of Chinese versions translated from the Buddhist sutras. However, there was very little in them about the commandments. How to bring the complete classics of Buddhist sutras, including the commandments, into China was a question of great concern for the Buddhists. Fa Xian was a monk who took this as his aim in going west to obtain sutras. In 399, he and several schoolmates left Chang'an for India to seek after the classic Buddhist commandments.

Fa Xian and his party passed through the State of Xiqin (today's Lanzhou in Gansu Province), State of Nanliang (east of today's Xining in Qinghai Province), and then arrived at Zhangye. In 440, they went further west, passing Dunhuang and the Liusha River, where there was not a single bird or animal. They could not tell their direction but only had bones as landmarks. They continued westward and finally arrived in India. After reaching India, Fa Xian studied there for three years. Once he obtained the sutra of commandments, he returned to China. Altogether he traveled in about 30 countries and returned to China by merchant boat. He was later in charge of the translation of sutras in Jiankang (today's Nanjing).

After Fa Xian, Xuan Zang (602-664) of the Tang Dynasty was another great translator and cultural envoy for peace in the history of the cultural exchanges between China and India. He made outstanding contributions to the cultural exchanges between China and the states of the western regions, especially India.

The main purpose of Xuan Zang's going to India was to solve an internal question of Buddhist ideology. Over some 400 years of evolvement after this religion came to China, Buddhism had witnessed great development there. However, the Buddhist theoretical system was huge with many different schools and complicated dogmas. When it came to China, there were already many different schools. In the early 7th century, the Buddhists in China began to discuss the questions of mind-nature and Buddha-mind. There were no intact theoretical explanations in the sutras. It was therefore necessary to go to India to solve the issue. That was one of the motivations for Xuan Zang going to India.

Around the autumn of 627, Xuan Zang departed Chang'an on his trip to India. The journey to India was as hard and rough as it had been for Fa Xian. Xuan Zang arrived at Qin Prefecture (today's Tianshui in Gansu Province), then went to Liangzhou (today's Wuwei in Gansu Province), and then to Lanzhou. After going through the Yumen Pass, he proceeded to Yiwu (today's Hami in Xiangjiang Uygur Autonomous Region). This section of the trip was extremely perilous because he had to pass through several hundred kilometers of desolated desert. Overcoming unimaginable difficulties, Xuan Zang arrived in Yiwu. The king of Yiwu treated him with hospitality. Xuan Zang stayed there for some ten days and then went on to Gaochang.

In the State of Gaochang, Xuan Zang was given a great courtesy. Out of political considerations, the king of

Xuan Zang going on a pilgrimage to India for Buddhist scriptures

Gaochang wanted to keep Xuan Zang around because he respected his broad knowledge and great personality. Xuan Zang declined the hospitality, saying, "The reason I am risking my life to go to India to seek for sutras is that I want to spread Buddhism in China. If I stay here, I will go back on my word and moreover it will impede the dissemination of Buddhism." The king of Gaochang had to agree with him and let him go on westward. The king also provided him with many provisions for his travel as well as a letter of credentials for him to use in going through the passes. This made Xuan Zang's travel more convenient. Seeing each other off, they agreed that Xuan Zang would come back by way of Gaochang. When Xuan Zang was about to return to China, he could have gone by the sea route. However, in order to keep his promise, he returned by the same overland route. But he did not go to Gaochang after he learned that the State of Gaochang had fallen to an enemy.

Xuan Zang arrived in northern India (today's Kashmir) in 628. He studied there for as long as 11 years. He traveled to many places in India to learn about the main schools of Buddhism. He won the respect and trust of Siladitya in central India. At the Kumbha Mela (the great festival of pilgrims usually held at a river bank), he was recommended to be the main speaker in responding to the theoretical challenges by different schools of Buddhism in India. He did so and was the final winner. Xuan Zang returned to Liyul in 643 and returned to Chang'an in early 645.

While Xuan Zang was in central India, Siladitya learned about the Tang Dynasty under the reign of Emperor Li Shiming through merchants from various countries in the western regions, so he inquired of Xuan Zang for more details. Then Siladitya sent an envoy to the Tang Dynasty in 641 to open a path for friendly exchanges between the two countries. Li Shiming also sent an envoy to India in return and then sent another envoy to India in 646. Afterwards, some Chinese monks came to India, so the cultural and peaceful exchanges continued.

3. Peace Through Marriage

In traditional society, military strength often determined the fate of a nation. The Chinese nation in the past created many political methods for handling relations between the Hans and the bordering nationalities, so as to resolve contradictions. "Peace through marriage" — a political marriage — was one of these. Because politics is a human social action, so power counts. Whether the policy of "peace through marriage" was effective or not was determined by the strength, especially the military strength of the two sides that were involved in the marriage. When China, with the Han people in power, was relative weak in military strength, "peace through marriage" could not bring peace. But, when the Han people were in power with political strength, the Chinese people adopted the political approach of "peace through marriage" instead of a policy of killing the bordering nationalities. This policy of keeping good relations with other ethnic groups shows fully the cultural tradition of the peace-loving Chinese people. Some emperors of the Han Dynasty (206 B.C.-220 A.D.) and the Tang Dynasty (618-907) carried out the policy of "peace through marriage" while they were in power, and this maintained peace on the border for a time and played a positive role in the cultural development of society. Though the policy of "peace through marriage" could not fundamentally solve all problems, it might relieve the contradictions and conflicts between nationalities for a certain period of time and expand the cultural exchanges between the Han people and bordering ethnic groups. Historically speaking, the Chinese nation had quite an advanced culture before the 17th century. The use of "peace through marriage" to spread science and technology was effective as well as a peaceful way to disseminate their advanced culture.

(1) Policy of "Peace Through Marriage" in the Han Dynasty

The policy of "peace through marriage" did not start during the Han Dynasty, but the theory took shape earlier during the Spring and Autumn Period. According to the *Remarks of Monarchs*, Zhang Wenzhong, a minister of the State of Lu, once said to Duke Zhuang of the State of Lu, "In order to win support from neighboring states, it is necessary to strengthen the relations between two states through marriage and the cementing of alliances. These are two methods that the state should take at the critical juncture." The success of the policy of "peace through marriage" during the Han Dynasty depended fundamentally on the comparison of the military strength between the Han Dynasty and the Huns. The vast grassland in northern China was the big arena inhabited by various nomadic tribes in northern China. During the later period of the Warring States Period, many of these tribes formed alliances within different regions. The Huns rose in the 3rd century B.C., the late Warring States Period, and fell in the 1st century A.D., the period of the Eastern Han Dynasty. The establishment of the political power of the Huns ended the scattered nomadic situation of tribes in northern China. They were thus the first to establish a unified political power in the whole of northern China. When the military force of the Han Dynasty had an upper hand, marriages between the Han Dynasty and the Huns brought tranquility to the borders. When the military force of the Han Dynasty was not as great as that of the Huns, such marriages did not bring peace. This does not mean that the policy of peace through marriage of the Han Dynasty was not effective, but only that it was effective within a certain scope.

In 200 B.C., Liu Bang, the founding emperor of the Han Dynasty was encircled by the Huns in Baideng (around today's Yanggao in Shanxi Province) and was almost killed. After he broke through the encirclement, he took his ministers' advice in arranging a marriage with the Huns. He first planned to send one of his princesses to King Maodun, the king of the Huns, for the proposed marriage. Yet because of the objection of the imperial families, he had to select a girl from an ordinary family and provide her with many betrothal gifts. In later years, the Han Dynasty continued its policy of "peace through marriage." However, the Huns did not stop plundering at the borders of the Han Dynasty because of these marriages. The reason for this was that the material wealth from marriage was far less than what they were able to obtain from plunder on the borders. Because the military strength of the Han Dynasty was not as powerful as that of the Huns, the policy of peace through marriage failed to produce peace at the border for the Han Dynasty.

Under the reign of Emperor Wu of the Han Dynasty (140 B.C.-86 A.D.), the economic and military strength of the Dynasty had its best days. In order to eliminate military threats from the Huns, Emperor Wu three times sent General Wei Qing and General Huo Qubing to the border to attack them. At the same time, he tried by every means possible to break a path through to the western regions by making an alliance through marriage with the State of Osun. Because the Han Dynasty under the reign of Emperor Wu was powerful, the "peace through marriage" solution had a totally different result from that of the early Han Dynasty. The Han Dynasty told the State of Osun to send an envoy with betrothal gifts before the king of Osun could marry a princess they would provide. At that time, the king of Osun, fearing an invasion by the Huns, sent an envoy to the Han Dynasty who expressed the willingness of the king to marry a princess of the Han Dynasty. So Emperor Wu provided two princesses for marriage. These were Princess Xijun and Princess Xieyou, both from the imperial family.

Princess Xieyou, in contrast to Princess Xijun, who was sad and under stress all day long because of the language barrier and her nostalgia, seemed more understanding of her political mission in the marriage. She lived for over 50 years in the State of Osun. In 75 B.C., the Huns built up their troop strength in preparation for an invasion of the State of Osun. Princess Xieyou immediately wrote a letter to the emperor of the Han Dynasty asking for military assistance. In 72 B.C. the Han Dynasty dispatched a force of 150,000 cavalry soldiers. They battled the Huns from five directions inflicting telling blows on the Huns.

Princess Xieyou had a deep understanding of the political function of marriage. She married her daughter to King Jiangbin of Qiuci (Kuqa), an event that has become somewhat legendary. Princess Xieyou had earlier sent her daughter to study Chinese music in the Han Dynasty. Upon the completion of these studies, the daughter set out to return to the State of Osun. On her way through Quici, she was detained by the State of Quici. The king of Quici had previously sent a representative to the State of Osun to propose that he be able to marry the daughter of Princess Xieyou, but this had been declined. Now the king of Quici made the proposal again. Out of political and diplomatic considerations, Princess Xieyou agreed to the marriage. After marrying her daughter to the king of Quici, Princess Xieyou asked that her daughter be allowed to accompany the family on a pilgrimage to the Han Dynasty. Clever Emperor Xuan agreed with the request of Princess Xieyou and conferred the title of princess on her daughter. Thereafter, the State of Quici developed a closer relationship with the Han Dynasty. Afterwards, the king of Quici went to the Han emperor on several occasions to give congratulations. In the meantime he brought back clothes and the ritual system of the Han Dynasty, as well as its building construction techniques. After the death of Jiangbin, his son claimed to be a grandson of the Hans and he maintained close relations with the Han Dynasty.

Princess Xieyou had a maid named Feng Liao, who was capable and well educated. She, with a diplomatic letter from the princess, traveled in the cities of the State of Osun and neighboring states to spread the culture of the Han Dynasty. She won the trust and respect of the people of Osun and the neighboring states. So they respectfully called her Madam Feng.

In 51 B.C., the aged and nostalgic Princess Xieyou, with the consent of the emperor, went back to be with the Han Dynasty with one of her grandsons and three of her granddaughters. She then returned at the age of over 70, to complete more than 50 years of living in the State of Osun.

During the later years of the Western Han Dynasty, there were internal splits within the Hun tribes as they moved westward. They were then separated into five kingdoms. In 53 B.C. Huhanxie, a king of one of the five kingdoms that was closest to the political territory of the Han Dynasty, proposed an alliance with the Han Dynasty. In 33 B.C., the emperor of the Han Dynasty agreed to the request of Huhanxie to marry Wang Zhaojun, one of the emperor's courtesans, in order to resume the policy of "peace through marriage." For over 100 years thereafter, the Han Dynasty had a peaceful relationship with the Huns. It wasn't until Wang Mang, who usurped power during the late Han Dynasty and implemented an erroneous policy toward the nationalities, that the peaceful situation was broken.

Wang Zhaojun was a daughter from a family of commoners. She had been selected to be a courtesan as she was beautiful and elegant. According to folklore, when Emperor Xuan of the Han Dynasty was selecting courtesans to be married to Huns so as to produce friendly relations between the two nationalities, he asked the imperial painter to draw portraits of each of them. Because Wang Zhaojun did not bribe the painter, the painter intentionally drew an ugly portrait of her. As a result, the emperor selected Wang Zhaojun for such a marriage. However, before she was about to leave, the emperor saw Wang Zhaojun in person and regretted his choice because she was so beautiful. He then wanted to exchange her for another courtesan. But Wang Zhangjun, knowing her mission and placing the interest of the nation first, persuaded the emperor by saying that she was willing to be married to a Hun in the north. The story of Wang Zhaojun has come down through history in China.

After she was married to King Huhanxie, Wang Zhaojun gave birth to a son. In 31 B.C., King Huhanxie died and Diaotao Mogao became the king. At the order of Emperor Cheng of the Han Dynasty, Wang Zhaojun, following the custom of the Huns, became the wife of the new king and gave birth to two daughters. Then, during the reign of Emperor Ai (6-2 B.C.), Wang Mang who held the real power of the Han Dynasty and in order to please the empress, asked the Huns to send back the eldest daughter of Wang Zhaojun so that she could wait upon the empress. Because Wang Mang thus interfered with the internal affairs of the Huns and undermined the relations between the Han Dynasty and the Huns, wars soon broke out in the north. In spite of this, the younger daughter of Wang Zhaojun and her husband did their utmost to produce good relations between the Han Dynasty and the Huns. In 14 A.D., the couple sent an envoy to the border to locate their uncle Wang Xi (elder brother of Wang Zhaojun), to talk about possible friendly relations. Because Wang Mang adhered to the erroneous policy, this act did not win genuine trust from the Huns. Though there was no war, small-scale harassments and plundering never ceased.

Wang Zhaojun was buried on the south bank of the Dahei River in today's Inner Mongolia. Her tomb is still there. The following epitaph is on the tombstone: "Devoted all to the north desert, She has brought peace to the border for generations. Her merits were as great as those of Huo and Wei." The names Huo and Wei are references to Huo Qubing and Wei Qing, two great generals of Emperor Wǔ who led expeditions against the Huns. To compare the merits of Wang Zhaojun with that of the two generals shows how highly people thought of Wang Zhaojun and her merit in bringing peace between nationalities at the expense of her personal interests.

Naturally, during the process of co-existence with neighboring ethnic groups, the politicians of Chinese traditional society did some foolish things. A typical example was that Empress Lü, wife of Emperor Liu Bang, who was in power for 16 years after her son succeeded to the throne. She took a closed view of cultural dissemination by stopping advanced techniques in farming and iron-casting from being spread to the minority ethnic groups, and even the animals sent to them were just males. This extremely erroneous policy regarding cultural exchanges led to resistance by the minority ethnic groups at the borders and the relations were tense for quite a while. After taking the throne, Emperor Wen immediately changed the closed policy and relations between the Han Dynasty and the minority ethnic groups became harmonious once more. During the late Western Han Dynasty, Wang

Mang adopted an erroneous policy in regard to the Huns and undermined the peace of over 100 years that had been in effect since the time of Emperor Xuan. As Wang took power, he hoped to set up his authority and used hard political means to interfere in the internal affairs of the Huns. This caused strong resentment and complaints against the Han people. Wang Mang also established an erroneous foreign policy toward the states in the western regions and they were forced to surrender to the Huns. Without reviewing this erroneous foreign policy and policy on nationalities, Wang Mang, determined to assert his authority regardless of the opposition of his generals, decided to lead 300,000 troops in attacking the Huns. As a result, this made his political power unstable.

(2) Policy of "Peace Through Marriage" and Peaceful Cultural Exchanges with the Tubo People During the Tang Dynasty

The peaceful exchanges between the Tang Dynasty and the Tubo (ancient Tibetan kingdom) people first naturally depended on the advanced culture and powerful military strength of the Tang Dynasty. However, the efforts of two princesses as envoys in their "peace through marriage" deserve credit. Under the reign of Emperor Taizong (627-650) of the Tang Dynasty, Princess Wencheng was sent as an envoy to Tubo in order to pioneer the peace cause between the Tang Dynasty and the Tubo people, to promote peace between the Han people and the Tubo people, and to provide cultural development and help the Tubo people create their own written language. In 684, Princess Jincheng was married in Tubo to further strengthen the friendly relations between the Han and the Tubo people.

Before the Tang Dynasty there were no exchanges between the hinterland of China and Tubo. The Tubo people made their living as nomads by raising yaks, horses, pigs, and camels, and they also planted barley and buckwheat. In the 7th century, Tri Songtsen became the king of Tubo, and he was then called Songtsen Ganpo. Songtsen Ganpo was a valiant leader. He led his army to unify many tribes on the Qinghai and Tibet plateau and established a powerful kingdom centered at Lhasa. After Songtsen Ganpo became the king, many states in the western regions came under his control. The marriage of Princess Wencheng to Songtsen Ganpo was a political tactic following the Tang army's defeat of Tubo. In 638, Songtsen Ganpo led the Tubo army in an attack on the border city of Songzou (today's Songpan County in Sichuan Province) of the Tang Dynasty. Emperor Taizong sent his troops to defeat them at Songzou. Songtsen Ganpo then declared himself a subject of the Tang Dynasty because he admired it for its prosperity. As he sent a letter of admitting his mistake in attacking Songzou, he proposed that a marriage might be arranged with the Tang Dynasty.

At first, Emperor Taizong did not agree to this, but later he decided to accept the proposal on the basis of political considerations for long time peace and security. The emperor selected a daughter of one of the imperial families who was well educated and named her Princess Wencheng. She was the daughter of a duke who was a distant relative of Emperor Taizong. She was beautiful and sedate and had received a very good schooling. Though she had doubts about going to far-away Tubo, she had to do so because she could not resist an order of the emperor and it was her political mission. After two months' preparation, in the fall of 641, a grandiose entourage was dispatched to escort the Princess Wencheng to Tubo. The procession included a great dowry, books, musical instruments, silk, and seeds. Her train also consisted of her maids, some scholars, musicians, and farming technicians.

This was a result of the profound vision of Emperor Taizong. He felt that it would ensure stability in the southeastern border areas as long as he kept close cultural ties with Tubo. Therefore, "peace through marriage" was no longer just a simple political marriage but also a matter of economic and cultural assistance to Tubo. Tubo would thus feel grateful toward the Tang Dynasty and follow it, resulting in long and lasting peaceful relations with the Tubo people. Princess Wencheng shouldered the political mission of harmonizing the relationship by being married to Songtsen Ganpo, ruler of Tubo, and her entourage was sent with her to help her fulfill the task.

After Princess Wencheng got to Tibet, Songtsen Ganpo, with a view to expressing his respect to the princess of the Tang Dynasty, ordered the building of a splendid palace for her. The palace was designed after the style of the Tang Dynasty so as to make her feel at home. In order to have a more common understanding, Songtsen Ganpo took off his fur coat and put on silk clothes that the princess tailored for him. Besides this, he tried his best to learn to speak Chinese from the princess.

Living in Tubo for some time, Princess Wencheng also helped to change some of the habits of the local people. For example, the Tubo people used to have a traditional habit of putting paste on their faces with brown dirt to drive out evil and protect them from demons. This was neither good-looking nor comfortable. Because it was a traditional habit, nobody raised objections. Most of the Tubo people just did so routinely. Princess Wencheng believed it did no good, so she tactically aired her views to Songtsen Ganpo, who felt there was something in what she said. So he immediately sent out instructions to abolish the habit.

After settling down, the musicians who came with the princess to Tubo began to work. They did their utmost to play the most popular music of the Tang court. Songtsen Ganpo is said to have felt this was a heavenly treat. So he selected a group of intelligent Tubo boys and girls to learn from the musicians. The music of the Han gradually spread throughout the region.

The scholars helped to sort out and file Tubo documents so as to keep a record of Songtsen Ganpo's important speeches to his ministers. Songtsen Ganpo instructed the children of his ministers and noble families to learn about Chinese culture and to study the books Princess Wencheng had brought with her. He also sent group after group of children of noble families to Chang'an, the capital of the Tang Dynasty, to study the classics there. When they returned they brought back Chinese culture.

The farming technicians planted the seeds they had brought to the fertile land of the plateau. After careful irrigation and fertilization, the crops produced a high yield. This helped the Tubo people learn the advanced farming techniques of the Han people. The Tubo people had planted barley and buckwheat but had a low yield because of poor management. At the order of Songtsen Ganpo and Princess Wencheng, the technicians taught their agricultural techniques to the local people in a planned way. This upgraded their farming techniques. They also taught them how to raise silkworms, and gradually, the Tubo people began to produce their own silk products.

Princess Wencheng also helped Songtsen Ganpo carry out political reform, and enabled Tubo to make unprecedented progress in the military, political, economic and cultural fields. Soon Tubo became the most powerful state in the western regions, which also served as a stronghold for the Tang Empire in the west.

In 648, Emperor Taizong sent an envoy named Wang Xiance to Tibet for the purpose of further strengthening friendship and seeing Princess Wencheng so as to fortify her position in Tibet. Unfortunately he was way-laid by some Indians and a great deal of silk, books and so on were seized. When he got to Tibet, he recounted the event to Songtsen Ganpo, who then sent a large number of troops to attack Indians and destroyed their capital, captured the prince of the ancient India, and saved Wang's entourage.

In 649, Emperor Taizong passed away and Emperor Gaozong succeeded the throne. The new emperor conferred the title of King of the Western Pre-fecture on Songtsen Ganpo and sent a special envoy with large quantity of silver, gold, silk, books, and seeds to the Tubo. He also sent some make-up and decorations especially for Princess Wencheng in recognition of her merits.

Songtsen Ganpo wrote a letter of gratitude to express his loyalty, saying, "On the occasion of Your Excellency taking the throne, I will bring my army to help put down those subordinates who dare to show disloyalty." In the meantime, he sent 15 kinds of treasures as sacrifices to be placed in front of the tomb of Emperor Taizong in order to convey his condolences. Emperor Gaozong was moved by Songtsen Ganpo's loyalty, and so he promoted him to King of Bin with a reward of 3,000 rolls of colored cloth. It was an eye-opener for the envoy of Tubo when he saw the prosperous scene of the Tang Dynasty at Chang'an. Taking the opportunity when Emperor Gaozong was much pleased, he pleaded for knowledge of the technique in brewing, rice-husking, and paper-making. The emperor agreed with all his requests. Along with the promoting of "peace through marriage" of the Princess Wencheng, the relationship between the Tang Dynasty and Tubo exhibited good chemistry.

After the demise of Songtsen Ganpo, his successor had worsening re-lations with the neighboring State of Tuguhun. Both rulers wrote letters to the Tang Dynasty to ask for a judgment. Because Emperor Gaozong, shilly-shallied and delayed in making such a judgment, the king of Tubo could no longer wait and sent out troops to defeat the State of Tuguhun. This action irritated Emperor Gaozong, and he then sent out a punitive expedition against Tubo. But the expedition was not successful. The troops of the Tang Dynasty were defeated. And after that, the Tubo attacked at the border of Tang Dynasty territory for a number of years and the situation remained hostile.

In the 30 years from the early spring of 641 when Princess Wencheng was married to Songtsen Ganpo to 670 when Emperor Gaozong sent the troops in a punitive expedition against Tuto, Tubo had very close relations with the Tang Dynasty. This was mainly because of the efforts of Princess Wencheng. There were no skirmishes at the borders in the western region and the advanced culture of the Han people was spread in Tubo. Then, because of the erroneous foreign policy and offhand resort to arms by Emperor Gaozong, the harmonious situation that Emperor Taizong and Princess Wencheng had nurtured was undermined. In 680 Princess Wencheng died of illness in Lhasa. The court of the Tang Dynasty sent a special envoy to express mourning but this failed to improve relations.

However, the Tubo people did not ignore the contributions made by Princess Wencheng because of the worsening of relations with the Tang Dynasty. After the death of Princess Wencheng, the Tubo people set up monasteries in many places in commemoration of her. The scholars and technicians who had followed her were treated well and when they died they were buried beside the tomb of Princess Wencheng. Today, the Tibetan people still regard Princess Wencheng and these friendly cultural envoys as saints.

During the 40 years between 670, when the Tang Dynasty troops were defeated by the Tubo, and 709, relations between the Tang Dynasty and Tubo witnessed many twists and turns of war and negotiations that inflicted great suffering on the peoples. In 708, the Tang Dynasty declined a Tubo envoy's proposal. At that time, some of the Chinese ministers objected to sending the Tibetan envoys home because they feared that that the group would not provide a report favorable to the Tang Dynasty if they were allowed to return. But Emperor Zhongzong said, "China should make relations with foreigners through trust" and he ordered that they be permitted to return.

In 709, the grandmother of Tri Tsugtsen, the 8-year-old king of Tubo, again sent an envoy to propose a Chinese marriage for the king. Emperor

Zhongzong, for political considerations, agreed with the proposal. He provided the daughter of Li Shouli of the imperial family, Princess Jincheng, to be the bride of King Tri Tsugtsen. In consideration of the young age of the new king, Emperor Zhongzong gave him several thousand rolls of silk and a group of technicians and musicians to accompany Princess Jincheng to Tubo.

Li Xian, Emperor Zhongzong, was under the control of his mother, Wu Zetian, for a long time and was even dethroned by his mother. After the death of his mother, he again took the throne. He was an emotional emperor with many hobbies. He and his wife organized courtesans and imperial maids in a tug-of-war contest. He disguised himself when making many inspections in his empire. He became sad after Princess Jincheng was married in Tubo. In the fourth lunar month of the next year (710), he went to Shiping County, the hometown of Princess Jincheng. There he led his ministers and Tubo envoys in a drinking party. While drinking, he became quite emotional and erupted into tears. He waived the county tax for one year and changed its name from Shiping County to Jincheng County, and changed the name of the town to Phoenix Pool, and the village to Sad-departure Village. Tubo also attached great importance to the marriage and built a palace exclusively for Princess Jincheng.

Nevertheless, this marriage for peace was different from the one involving Princess Wencheng. The Tubo did not have the strength to invade eastward and their internal political situation was not stable. On the surface they took the initiative to propose peace but actually maintained their resentment against the Tang Dynasty. Making use of the marriage for peace, they asked for more land. They requested the area of Hexi Jiuqu (today's Hexi Corridor in Gansu) as a "swimming pool" for Princess Jincheng. It was a land of ample water and fine grass for raising cattle and sheep at the border of the Tang Dynasty territory. In anticipation of building a stronger peace, the Tang Dynasty generously agreed with this almost unreasonable request. But afterwards, Tubo became more inclined to invade the western territories of the Tang Dynasty.

On the fourth year of Princess Jincheng's marriage to the Tubo king (714), Tubo wrote letters to the Tang Dynasty that proposed the drawing of boundaries. At the same time, the king led 100,000 troops in an attack on the borders of the Tang Dynasty and forced the Tang Dynasty general, Yang Shouju, to commit suicide. General Yang had escorted Princess Wencheng to Tubo and then he was stationed at the border. Emperor Xuanzong was outraged by this attack and decided to lead the army in fighting back. He defeated the Tubo army. Afterwards, the Tang Dynasty sent an envoy to console Princess Jincheng. Tubo sent envoys to mourn over the dead soldiers and asked for equal co-existence from the Tang Dynasty. In the meantime, Princess Jincheng wrote to the Tang Dynasty asking that they accept the Tubo's request for peace and pass on the message that the Tubo king and ministers would like to sign a peace alliance and engrave their good-will in stone.

At that time, the Tubo's king was still young and the military and political power was in the hands of his ministers. Though there was the marriage for peace, there were still frequent skirmishes at the border. In the later wars between the Tang Dynasty and Tubo, the Tang Dynasty always won. So the Tubo king sent people to the Tang Dynasty to ask for peace. Emperor Xuanzong at first did not approve of this, but later he took the advice of his ministers and agreed to the Tubo's request for peace. He sent his envoy to Tubo to have Princess Jincheng tell the Tubo's king of his wish to handle the border issue peacefully. The king was quite pleased and brought forth all the documents and letters of friendly exchanges between the two countries since the time of Emperor Taizong. He gave gifts to the envoy of the Tang Dynasty and sent his own envoy to the Dynasty with a letter to express his desire for peace.

After these mutual visits, Tubo presented a gift at the border town of Chiling of a large herd of horses and asked in return some Chinese cultural classics and the "Five Books." The Tang Dynasty gave these to them. Both sides drew a borderline with inscribed stones at Chiling. However, since Tubo's strength was increasing and it continued to annex small neighboring states that were friendly with the Tang Dynasty, military frictions between the Tang Dynasty and Tubo never ceased. In 723, Princess Jincheng passed away. The next year, Tubo sent people to inform the Tang Dynasty of her death and asked for peace. Yet because of the old grudges, the Tang Dynasty would not agree to this request for peace. The war between the Tang Dynasty and Tubo continued to advance until the fall of the Tang Dynasty.

There were times of peace and of wars, but the threat of Tubo to the Tang Dynasty never abated. So the system of "peace through marriage" ended.

The Tang Dynasty continued a policy of war and peace with neighboring nations. The consequence of the wars was losses on both sides. Though "peace through marriage" did not bring lasting peace, yet it intensified contacts and understanding with the Tubo people during the short periods of peace. Later, war and peace took place one after the other, but the alliances between the two was always involved with the policy of "peace through marriage." This shows that cultural exchanges in the form of marriages for peace were conducive to the mutual understanding between the two countries. Particularly, the Tubo people rapidly developed into a powerful state after they absorbed the advanced culture of the Tang Dynasty. This also shows that the peaceful and cultural exchanges of the Tang Dynasty had a positive influence on the nationalities on the western borders. Of course, we should have a historical view of the relations in ancient China with the minority ethnic groups at the borders. In the heyday of the Tang Dynasty, the government adopted a policy of military occupation in the areas of the neighboring nationalities, leading to tense relations with the minority nationalities on the eastern borders. Its use of force against Korea in the east and its war with the Tubo and the Hui people in the west led to great financial losses to the Tang Dynasty. As a result, the Tang Dynasty exhausted its strength through war. Along with internal and external troubles, the Tang Dynasty gradually fell.

The wars at the borders and national contradictions 1,300 to 1,400 years ago have been buried in the tomb of history. However, in looking through history, we may discern the basic insight in the process of exchanges among nationalities, namely, only by adopting a cultural policy for national peace, can the nation bring about political stability and economic prosperity.

4. "Treating Those from Afar Who Are not Convinced"

The Confucian advocacy of using literal virtue was a political form of natural persuasion. The so-called "using literal virtue to treat those from afar who are not convinced" meant, as Mencius put it, to address relations with other states centered on benevolent governance. Through the later reform of the ancient political principle in dealing with states of the dukes during the Spring and Autumn Period, it developed into a principle of cultural exchanges for peace in the international community.

(1) Confucian Thinking of World Outlook on "Benevolent Governance" and World Peace

The Confucian belief is that "benevolent governance" is more of an ideal for a political form in a harmonious world than a conceptual description of the real social political situation. The core spirit of this is to establish an ideal society for other nations to follow so as to achieve a situation of world peace. Though the definition of the world of Confucians is far away from that of the modern sense of the world, the thinking toward peaceful co-existence among the big communities of mankind contained within it bears an instructive import for world peace today.

The Confucian political ideal contains a kind of benevolent governance. In criticizing Ran You and Zi Lu, two of Confucius' disciples, for their assistance to Jishi in attacking a dependent state, Confucius put forward the political ideal of drawing smaller states closer through virtue. He said, "If they do not yield to your authority, you should upgrade your cultural prestige so that they will follow automatically. Since they come to you by your persuasion, you should let them be at ease." This thinking emphasized that advanced and civilized countries should pull together other countries so that they could learn and participate through inspiration rather than use war to push forward their civilization. Therefore, this concept bears strong current significance. Because the promotion of peace means to solve disputes among states, Confucius especially praised Guan Zhong by saying, "It was Guang Zhong's personal political ability to unite dukes instead of relying on the force of war chariots. What a great virtue of benevolence! What a great virtue of benevolence!"

In ritual culture, the loyalty of a minister to his king was extremely important. Guan Zhong once served as a teacher and political adviser to Gong Zijiu (elder brother of Duke Huan of the State of Qi). In contention over the throne of the kingdom, Duke Huan killed Gong Zijiu. Zhao Hu, another teacher and political adviser to Gong Zijiu committed suicide, but Guan Zhong did not and instead became prime minister for the Duke Huan of Qi. Therefore, some people criticized Guan Zhong for his disloyalty. But Confucius confirmed the political action of Guan Zhong who later chose to join Duke Huan of Qi, and he defended this political choice. He said, "Guan Zhong assisted Duke Huan of Qi to stand strong among the dukes and correct everything under heaven. Even today people are still enjoying the benefits brought about through him. Without Guan Zhong we might have become a backward nation. Why should he have acted like ordinary folk in observing trivial rites and loyalties and ended his life in a mountain gully and remained unknown?" The reason Confucius defended Guan Zhong was that Guan Zhong assisted the State of Qi in maintaining its advanced political culture of benevolent governance instead of using force. His great historical merit much overweighed his political disloyalty to one person. One can see from this example that the Confucian ideology in politics did not simply emphasize a minister's loyalty to the king but also upheld the belief that loyalty should be subject to a higher cultural value — the cultural ideal of the politics of benevolent governance.

Mencius, another great thinker of the Confucian school, believed that benevolent governance was a political ideal that was not hard to realize. As Mencius put it, "You will have plenty of grain, if you farm according to the seasons; you will have plenty of fish and turtles for food, if you fish with a loosely-woven net; you will have plenty of timber, if you go up the mountain to fell trees at an appropriate time. People will live a happy life with plenty of food, fish, and timber. This is the beginning of benevolent governance."

In the thinking of Mencius, benevolent governance was the ideal political situation. In order to realize such benevolent governance, a duke of a small kingdom might also be a king for all under heaven. The fundamental political measure was to implement benevolent governance. "When all officials want to serve under you, when all farmers want to farm on your land, when all businessmen want to do business in your market, when all travelers want to go over your roads, and when all those with a grievance want to lodge their complaints to you," you, a duke, might become the king.

The concrete measures of benevolent governance put forth by Mencius might be epitomized in four respects: First, to ensure a solid economic foundation of society (Mencius: "In a state where people of seventy are clothed in floss silk garments, and have meat to eat, and the masses do not suffer from hunger or cold...."); second, to respect the life and property of people (Mencius: "It is the protection of the people; with this a ruler can not be prevented from winning the unification of the world."); third, to care for every member of society just as you care for the old and young of your family (Mencius: "Do reverence to the elders in your own family and extend it to those in other families; show loving care to the young in your own family and extend it to those in other families."), and fourth, to do the things people are happy about and be concerned about the worries of people (Mencius: "The people will delight in the joy of a ruler who delights in their joy, and will grieve at the sorrow of a ruler who grieves at their sorrow.").

Mencius firmly believed in the concept that "benevolence is invincible." He said, "It is possible that a man who is not benevolent may have a dukedom, but it is impossible that he will have the recognition of the world." Therefore, benevolent governance became the political principle as well as the legal basis for the resources of power for governance.

Mencius was particularly opposed to expeditions or launching wars to seize land and people. In today's terms, Mencius was particularly opposed to grabbing wealth through war. He criticized Duke Hui of Liang for driving his people to war for the sake of more land in violation of the political principle of benevolence. He had a negative comment on the wars of the Spring and Autumn Period when saying "There was not a just war during the Spring and Autumn Period." The so-called "expedition" meant that the Emperor of the Zhou Dynasty launched an expedition against his dukedom, or a superior's expedition against his subordinates. One duke did not have the right to launch an expedition against another. If all the dukes ran affairs in line with benevolent governance, how could there be any wars? Mencius also made a philosophical analysis of the legal foundation for wars. His ideal of benevolent governance was this: "One should neither do any unjust thing nor kill any innocent person for the sake of running the world." According to the principles of the Confucian school, he separated benevolent governance from hegemony. Hegemony involves running things through force in the name of benevolence. Only a big power can make use of hegemony. Promoting benevolent governance with literal virtue resulted in benevolent governance, and this did not necessarily mean that only a big power could accomplish this. One may see that the politics of benevolent governance in Mencius' mind bore infinite just power.

Xun Zi, another great Confucian scholar before the Qin Dynasty, discussed the political issue of benevolent governance even more systematically. The book *Xun Zi* （《荀子》）dealt with how to solve disputes under the guidance of benevolent governance:

"The capable and intelligent may be upgraded; the useless may be discarded immediately; arch criminals may be executed immediately; the mediocre should be inspired without any official's teachings. Everything should be as clear as a father and son. Children of dukes or high-ranking officials should go into the ranks of the commoners if their behavior does not meet the requirements of rites. Children of common families may be promoted to high-ranking official positions if they have the right virtue through cultural accumulation and meet the requirements of rites. All those who slander, do evil and abnormal things, or make trouble should be educated and given time to turn their lives about. There should be rewards to encourage them and measures to punish them. Keep those who are content with their position, while dismissing those who are not. The state should take notice of the five categories of the handicapped and give them jobs according to their ability. The government should ensure their basic livelihood, without leaving anyone behind. Those whose behavior and capability violates the current government should be executed without amnesty. These are the celestial virtues or politics of benevolent governance."

Of course, what Xun Zi said was far different from the requirements of modern democratic politics; especially some of the political measures that are not in line with the modern principles of humanitarianism. However, considering that the value of ordinary people was universally ignored some 2,300 years ago, some of his political thinking was quite progressive.

Compared to Mencius, Xun Zi's ideas of benevolent governance more clearly embodied a civilized political form, which mainly consisted of the concrete content of the ritual system. The essence of civilization was centered on a spirit of benevolence. Comparing this spirit to hegemony in politics, Xun Zi held that benevolent governance should proceed as follows:

"Benevolence is above everything; justice is above everything; and prestige is above everything. When benevolence is above everything, everybody without exception will be close to the ruler. When justice is above everything, everyone will respect him. When prestige is above everything, no one will dare to make him an enemy. Relying on the invincible strength and political principle to conquer the hearts of people, he will be able to defeat anybody without waging wars and will possess the land without attacking others. Everybody is willing to be subordinate without having to mobilize armies. This is genuine benevolent governance."

In Xun Zi's thinking, the concrete approaches to the political ideal of benevolent governance were composed of the following three conditions. First, the politics of benevolent governance was based on a political model of the previous three dynasties. As Xun Zi put it that the cream of the political system of benevolent governance does not exceed the rational spirit of the system of the three dynasties of Xia, Shang, and Zhou, nor does it violate the rule of the current benevolent governance. It is also pointless to trace back beyond the three dynasties and it is neither graceful nor smooth if it violates the current rule of law.

Second, the realization of the ideal of benevolent governance needs a set of strict systems of rewards and punishments. Xun Zi believed: The order of the day in a society under benevolent governance is that those without virtue cannot enjoy a high position and respect; those without capability cannot become officials; those without merit cannot be rewarded, and those who have not committed any crime will not be punished. No one accidentally acquires officialdom in the dynasty. No criminal can accidentally escape the punishment of law. The talented and those with morals will be given greater responsibility according to their virtue. Good citizens will be separated from the bullies who will be checked, but the punishment should not be severe. The common folk know that those who do well in a family will be rewarded by the dynasty. Those who secretly do evil things will be punished openly. This is the rule of norms and the rule of benevolent governance.

Third, in realizing benevolent governance, it is necessary to formulate reasonable political, economic, and foreign trade policies so that the society is an open one. As Xun Zi put it that a benevolent ruler implements equal taxation, manages state affairs, and judges everything with an aim to nurture the people. Ten percent taxation is levied on farming land. The market is under supervision without taxation. Fishing in rivers and mountain lakes is encouraged or banned according to the seasons and without taxation. Different rates of taxation on farming land will be collected according to its fertility. Contributions to the imperial court are determined according to the distance of the place from the capital. There should be smooth transportation and the transfer of materials and cereals without delay. All in the four seas (world) are one family. Those who are close to the imperial court cannot hide their capability. Those who are far from the imperial court will not have extra burdens. No remote countries are beyond the influence of benevolent governance. Everyone who cherishes benevolent governance will be happy to abide by its rules and feel safe and satisfied.

Contrary to the political goal of hegemony, "to rule the country with benevolent governance" is to be enacted to win the will of the people of the country. So the position and dignity of human beings was the major concern of benevolent governance. That was why Xun Zi said: Benevolent governance contends for talented people. Hegemony contends for the countries of others. The powerful contends for the land of others. Making use of a dialogue between Yao and Shun, Xun Zi elaborated the political knack of how such benevolence can be won: One day, Yao said to Shun, "What should I do if I want all the people under the heaven to be my subjects?" Shun answered, "Concentrate on benevolence and virtue without making mistakes. Be careful that your actions make no error. Adhere to the virtue of loyalty and trust without breaching them. Then all the people under heaven will naturally come to you... Why should you rack your brains to find a way to make them subservient to you?"

The conversation shows that Xun Zi basically adhered to the thinking of literal virtue developed by Confucius on the issue of how to acquire the right to rule over the world. It requested that the ruler of a country should be loyal and trustworthy without any breaches in regard to all the people under him. It was roughly the same with the ideal of Confucius: "Use literal virtue to treat those from afar who are not convinced."

After the Han Dynasty, the concept of "benevolent governance" permeated many official documents and became the Chinese ideal for peace in world politics. The idea of unified benevolent governance was particularly promoted in books by Dong Zhongshu and He Xiu of the Eastern Han Dynasty. Combining this idea with that in *The Book of Rites* (《礼记》)，Kang Youwei developed and made supplementary additions to create the concept of "Great Harmony" in China's early ideology.

(2) National Independence in Cultural Exchanges

The essence of the "Chinese or foreign debate" in Chinese history was based on the desire for culturally backward nations to accept the principles of existence of the culturally advanced nations rather than on racial discrimination.

During the time of Confucius, the ritual system of the Zhou Dynasty was an advanced political system in comparison to that in neighboring nationalities. The main spirit of the "Chinese or foreign debate" of that time was to establish and maintain the prevailing position of the culture of central China and to adapt neighboring minority ethnic groups to it through the approach of "benevolent governance." After the introduction of Buddhism into China, the "Chinese or foreign debate" became a "contention between Chinese and Buddhist values," or chiefly the struggle between the teachings of the Confucian and Taoist schools with those of Buddhism for the position of a national religion. This round of the "Chinese or foreign debate" ended with the emergence of Zen Buddhism, or the Chinese form of Buddhism. The emergence of the new Confucian school of the Song and Ming dynasties (developed from the 10th century to the 17th century on the basis of the traditional Confucian ideology with the addition of many Buddhist ideas as well as those of Taoism) marked the Chinese culture as it developed its own national spirit. After the 13th century, the Mongol and Manchu ruling groups respectively defeated the rule of the Hans. Though there was national internal strife over daily routines, there was no genuine ideological debate about the Chinese or foreign ideas because they both gradually took up Confucian rites as the platform on which to run the country. After the 16th century, along with the arrival of Western missionaries in China and the introduction of Christianity and Western culture with a totally different spirit, the new round of debates on the matter of being Chinese or foreign gradually evolved into a contention between the Chinese and Western cultures.

As a matter of fact, throughout this period there were some farsighted thinkers who affirmed the strong points of the culture of minority ethnic groups and pointed out inadequacy of Chinese culture and criticized it for being overelaborate. Confucius once criticized Chinese culture for being at the brink of collapse and not as good as the practices between the kings and ministers of the minority ethnic groups. Gu Yanwu (1613-1682), a great thinker at the time between the Ming and Qing dynasties, affirmed a simple and effective administrative principle and criticized the overelaborating of Chinese culture, which, he believed, was the main cause of the decline of Chinese culture. He advocated learning from the minority ethnic groups. Therefore, on the issue of the "Chinese or foreign debate," Chinese culture does not always regard its own as superior, but has been open to learn from others by a comparison of the strong points and shortcomings.

The expressions of the "Chinese or foreign debate" emphasized different aspects at different times in history. Nevertheless, the theme was basically the same, e.g., how to establish the prevailing position of Chinese culture and foster national confidence. Naturally, in the process of the debate, there were some radical arguments, among which the typical ones were of two kinds: viewpoints of narrow centralism toward Chinese culture and the radical viewpoint of "changing China by using things foreign." Both viewpoints are a one-sided understanding of the process of cultural exchanges between China and foreign countries and were not conducive to the integration and development of cultures. Historical experience proved that the rational viewpoint toward Chinese or foreign should be based on national confidence and should boldly acquire the cultural cream of other nationalities. Only by doing so, could Chinese culture keep its vigorous vitality.

The issue originated a long time ago, as early as in the "Chapter Shun" of the *Collection of Ancient Texts* (《尚书·舜典》), and there was a distinctive disparaging of minority ethnic groups in *Zuo Zhuan*. The "Chinese or foreign debate" in the early days inclined toward Chinese national centralism.

The Confucian school, with Confucius in the lead, made theoretical corrections to the aforementioned viewpoint by emphasizing chiefly the achievements of the culture in central China and discarding racial bias. Its important theoretical foundation was based on the order of rites and exceeding the stage of primitive barbarian culture. So when Zi Gong, a student of Confucius, asked the teacher whether Guan Zhong could be counted as a man of benevolence, Confucius answered that he was indeed one and advised the student not to make a negative appraisal of Guan Zhong as the common people did. This was because Guan Zhong maintained the advanced life style of Chinese culture and helped to prevent the culture from deterioration.

On this important issue, with an outstanding viewpoint, Confucius spoke highly of the contributions made by Guan Zhong in preserving the advanced culture. He told his students not to be bothered too much by some of Guan Zhong's ordinary political activities that were not in line with the rites. He stressed the reforming impact of advanced culture over that of any backward one. He said, "Even if one were in an out-of-the-way place, it would not be remote so long as gentlemen were living there." What he meant by this was that gentlemen could educate the common folk in civilization. Some examples in later Chinese history drove home the point. For instance, Liu Zongyuan (773-819), a famous learned man of the Tang Dynasty was banished to Liuzhou in Guangxi, and Su Shi (1037-1101), a famous man of letters and painter of the Tang Dynasty, was banished to Hainan Island. They both made great contributions to the Chinese cultural development. According to historical records, after being banished to Hainan, Su Shi, without being downhearted, pushed the cause of local education and thus changed the backward situation of Hainan's culture.

Mencius basically followed the Confucian viewpoint on this issue. He believed that the Chinese could change foreign culture and not vice versa. He went so far as to say that Shun was a foreigner from the east while King Wen of Zhou was a foreigner from the west. They made great achievements in their lifetimes only because they had inherited the spirit of benevolent governance from the Chinese civilization. He therefore affirmed the superiority of Chinese civilization. From an abstract philosophical viewpoint, Mencius was not wrong. But his viewpoint was an inclination toward the centralism of Chinese civilization, and neglected the interaction between Chinese civilization and the neighboring minority ethnic cultures. To simplify the relationship of nations in the exchanges of human civilization and mutual learning as that of one replacing the other was not conducive to nations learning from each other.

Nevertheless, in about the 2nd century B.C., the Confucian viewpoint on this issue was greatly changed. *The Book of Rites* has quite an objective description of the customs of the different nationalities and presents the theoretical conclusion that humans have five basic requirements of housing, food, clothing, utilities, and tools, though the different nationalities have different customs. The author of the book believed that different nationalities might communicate through interpreters in their cultural exchanges, although they spoke different languages. *The Book of Rites* describes the history of harmonious relations between the Chinese nation and the neighboring ethnic groups after the Spring and Autumn and Warring States periods. This helped the Chinese to develop a more objective understanding of the cultural features of neighboring ethnic groups.

Around the time of the reign of Emperor Ming (58-76) of Eastern Han Dynasty, Buddhism began to spread into China. Thereafter, the theoretical center of the "Chinese or foreign debate" turned into a "Chinese or Buddhist debate." In this, there were viewpoints criticizing Buddhism as a contradiction against the Chinese tradition of rites as well as viewpoints that were combination of Confucianism, Taoism, and Buddhism. From the beginning, the "Chinese or Buddhist debate" exhibited a complicated situation. Anti-Buddhist theories in the early days were mainly matters of national prejudice based on an ignorance of Buddhism and Indian culture. This prejudice found concentrated expression in *On Theoretical Puzzling* (《理惑论》) by Mou Zi (written around the mid 2nd century). *On Theoretical Puzzling* revealed various prejudices in the form of questions and answers. In short, these prejudices can be roughly summed up in the following three ways. First, some Confucian scholars resented Buddhism because it advocated people becoming monks without caring for their parents. Second, the Confucian school emphasized that "there are three things which are considered unfilial, and the worst of them is to have no posterity," so Buddhism did not conform to the Chinese rites because it preached against marriage or promoted the leaving of one's wife. Third, Buddhism said that the death of a human being was the beginning of another life. It thus ran counter to Confucian atheism. Confucius said, "Till you have learnt to serve men, how can you serve ghosts? ...Till you know about the living, how are you to know about the dead?"

However, the author of *On Theoretical Puzzling* was not opposed to

Buddhism, but made a defense of Buddhism. He was the first to advocate the integration of Confucian, Taoist, and Buddhist concepts. Mou Zi believed that the tonsure of Buddhist believers had no great differences from that of the Yue people in the south. Moreover, there were some Buddhist warriors who died for justice. And they should not be criticized solely for a lack of filial loyalty. A genuine gentleman will do valiant deeds for justice. This put a new meaning into the moral concept of bravery and justice from that of the Confucian ideological definition of bravery and justice. He said there was nothing wrong with Buddhist believers who had their own concept of values without observing the rites of the Han Dynasty. Confucius never talked about spirits and ghosts, but the Confucian scholars of later days have all commemorated their ancestors on memorial occasions, while the Taoists have always paid special attention to the issue of life and death. Thus, he concluded, there was nothing wrong with the Buddhists believing in gods. These defending statements helped promote the dissemination of Buddhism in China.

The theoretical debates over Buddhism and traditional Confucianism and Taoism differentiated the impact of the Confucian and Buddhist classics on human society. In daily life Confucianism managed secular affairs while Buddhism took care of the affairs of the souls of humans. Different theories play different roles. Some enlightened scholars of the Wei and Jin dynasties (3rd-5th century) advocated the combining of Buddhism with Confucianism and Taoism. This performed a great role in promoting Chinese Buddhism.

During the Ming and Qing dynasties (14th-20th centuries), the "Chinese or foreign debate" further evolved into a debate between Chinese and Western culture. After Western missionaries represented by Matteo Ricci of Italy (1552-1610) came to China, a new round in the debate started. From the late 16th century to the Opium War of the 1840s, the debate consisted of two major viewpoints. One was an adherence to learning from each other and integration; the other was focused on maintaining the Chinese traditional rites and opposition to absorbing Western culture.

(a) School for integration represented by Xu Guangqi

Xu Guangqi (1562-1633), a great scientist of the late Qing Dynasty, saw the strong points of Western science in the early days of the encounter

Matteo Ricci and Xu Guangqi

between the Chinese and Western cultures, so he was determined to master Western science. Therefore he accepted a Christian baptism. His basic attitude was to make Western academic learning serve the Chinese politics of that time. He and Matteo Ricci translated a Western work, the *Theory of Geometry* (《几何原理》). He also came to recognize some of the shortcomings of Chinese science. Thus he put forth a viewpoint of cultural integration. He said, "It is necessary to integrate first before we can achieve excellence." In order to protect Christian missionaries, he searched for methods to defend their preaching, saying that the foreign missionaries wished to have everybody serve their god just as Chinese Confucianism wished to have everybody serve heaven. In other words, he said that they were about the same. The missionaries, he said, traveled from far away and overcame difficulties in order to make everybody with a kind heart satisfy the love of the god. Xu Guangqi and some other late comers such as scientists Wang Zheng, Mei Wending, and Fang Yizhi all promoted the integration of the Chinese and Western cultures. Even Emperor Shunzhi (1644-1662) and Emperor Kangxi (1662-1723) of the Qing Dynasty extolled Western science that could be used by China. Emperor Shunzhi gave an order to confer Johann Adam Schall von Bell, a German (1592-1666), with the title of adviser. Emperor Kangxi ordered the missionaries to work out geographical maps for him and established the Western royal institute within the imperial palace, which was similar to today's scientific research institute in the West. He also studied the Western knowledge of the calendar and mathematics.

(b) Opposition represented by Yang Guangxian

During the period of the late Ming and early Qing dynasties, some conservatives were opposed to Western science and culture, though other enlightened scholars emphasized the need to study them. Since 1610, Shen Quan of the Ming Dynasty wrote memorials three times to the imperial court criticizing Christianity.

After the memorials were submitted, some Western missionaries were arrested and their property was confiscated. The case of Yang Guangxian's opposition to the Western calendar was complicated. There were some personal interests and grudges as much as there were political considerations. On the whole his was a conservative viewpoint. Especially, he put forth the position, "I would rather have no good calendar than have the Westerner's one." In fact, he wanted to keep China closed, and as a consequence, this was not conducive to Chinese development. He criticized the Christian missionaries' activities in China for both cultural and political reasons. He believed first that the Christians deemed the Chinese to be a barbarian people, which was an insult to the Chinese people. Second, they made surveys of China's landscape, its mountains and rivers, and that they might have ulterior motives. He said that since the time of Matteo Ricci, missionaries used the teaching of their calendar to covertly preach religion, and they had established churches in 13 provinces. They collected information bit by bit, and China should guard against their political intentions. Of course, there was something in this viewpoint. However, we should never stop cultural and scientific exchanges between China and the West just for that reason. The best way to prevent an invasion of other nations was to learn from their strong points and make ourselves strong to ward off such worries.

Yang Guangxian's outlook cared little for the interests of the whole nation. On the surface, it was aimed to maintain the interests of the rulers, but actually it hastened the demise of the Qing Dynasty. In the end China fell into the passive position of being bullied. The calendar was related to a series of matters relating to agricultural production. How could the dynasty maintain its political rule if the material foundation was not solid? This viewpoint of a few short-sighted officials, superficially concerned for the interests of the empire, seriously obstructed the progress of the modern

Chinese people in learning about the advanced sciences and culture of the West. The narrow-minded viewpoint was one of the ideological causes that gradually led China into its 19th century decline.

In the conflict between different cultures, the debate over the Chinese and Western cultures did not lead to wars because the national strength of the Chinese dynasty was able to maintain its sovereignty. However, because of the influence of the conservatives, cultural exchanges between China and the West were impeded from both directions. One was from the conservatives of the Roman Church. They attempted to conduct cultural infiltration and economic invasion through religion, and the missionary activities were a clear interference into Chinese internal affairs. This finally led to resentment by the Chinese government and resulted in the suspension of scientific and cultural exchanges between China and the West. The other was from the conservative influence in the Chinese government. They adopted unjust means of the religious persecution of the Western missionaries and turned an ideological and conceptual debate into a political struggle. The process of historical development later regretfully went astray. Chinese people failed to grasp the fine opportunity in the 18th and 19th centuries to learn from the West. This led to almost a hundred years of hardship for China. The causes were complicated and the main lessons deserve to be studied.

The Opium War ended with China as the loser and the Qing Dynasty thus lost face. Even so, only a very few enlightened people awoke. Wei Yuan (1794-1857), a thinker of the late Qing Dynasty, was among these. He made use of the contents of a book titled *Countries of the Four Oceans* (《四海志》), written by Lin Zexu (1785-1850), as part of his own book, *Illustrations of Overseas Countries* (《海国图志》), in an attempt to awaken the Chinese people to developments in the outside world. In this book he said, "The purpose of my book is to overcome and subdue foreign things with things foreign and to learn from their strong points for the purpose of subduing things foreign." His statement "to learn from their strong points for the purpose to subduing things foreign" was a viewpoint relating to the exchanges between China and the West in the first stage of modern China. It had a strong hint of utilitarianism, but marked the fact that the modern Chinese people began to look squarely at Western culture. So it was a gratifying turning point.

The second stage was represented by Feng Guifen Wang Tao and Zheng Guanying, whose viewpoint was to "make Chinese learning as the base, Western learning for application." Feng Guifen said, "Using the Chinese ethics and classics as base, supplemented by other countries' means for getting rich and powerful." Zheng Guanying said, "Chinese learning serves as the body while Western learning serves as the approach. Taking Chinese learning as base and Western learning as the auxiliary will help us to know the priorities, review the changes, and use both soft and hard tactics to improve the political system. This is where learning lies." The viewpoint of these capitalist reformers in the early days became the famous ideological view of "making Chinese learning as the base, Western learning for application," which actually was closely linked with the viewpoint of maintaining the feudal and rigid empire. It was seriously criticized by Yan Fu after China was defeated in the Sino-Japanese War of 1894-1895. Yan Fu said, "The main body and means are all of one thing. An ox has a body, which serves as means to carry. A horse has a body, which serves to run. I have never heard that an ox serves as the body and a horse serves as means…. So Chinese learning has its body and means while the West has its own. The body and the means will be established if each differentiates the other, and both will die if they are mingled." Yan Fu's viewpoint gave telling blows to those conservatives who intended to maintain the old social system.

During the 20th century, Western culture flooded into China and a school for "Westernization" and a school of "national purists" emerged. When Marxism was introduced into China, the Chinese Marxists gave their answers to the issue of Chinese or Western, today and historically. In his work, *On New Democracy* (《新民主主义论》)，Mao Zedong put forward the idea of "making things foreign serve China." Due to the influence of the then international communist environment, the Chinese for a while deviated from their theoretical advocacy. Since the reform and opening up, China has put forth the concept of building China into a modern country with Chinese characteristics. This new viewpoint on Chinese and Western culture is, in principle, correct. However, it needs continuous and theoretical exploration as to how to carry out the theoretical theme to the letter. In retrospect, the rethinking and review of how the Chinese successfully learned and drew lessons from foreign cultures, its inadequacy and even failures in learning from foreign cultures should benefit the cultural exchanges today.

5. If Kings and Dukes Abide by Morals, Everything will Fall into Place

In Chinese ideological history, the Taoists put forth their exclusive philosophical thinking on the question of social harmony. They were strongly opposed to wars, tyranny, and the making and using of advanced weapons. They requested the rulers to attach importance to social morals, people's lives, and property, so as to provide a peaceful environment of happy living for the people. The political thinking of "valuing virtues and benevolence" put forth by Lao Zi and the political tactics of cherishing softness, mercy, and frugality were valuable resources for human society in maintaining peace.

In Lao Zi's philosophy, human recognition of the value of peace is a fundamental mark of wisdom. He put forward a famous idea that if one understood peace, he mastered the normal rules, and if one mastered the normal rules, he possessed wisdom. He gave a vivid example from daily life to illustrate the full expression of harmony. He said: Look at the baby who cries many times in a day. Its body never shows any signs of injury because of the cries. Why is this so? It is because its internal harmony has reached its natural extreme. If people could realize the value of a harmonious situation, they would be able to master the normal rules. If one is able to master the normal rules, one will possess wisdom. If people intentionally raise their lives, their bodies would be vulnerable to disasters. If one does his utmost to intensify his desire, it would mean flaunting his superiority. These ways of doing things run counter to the fundamental rule of harmony, and as a result only accelerate one's death.

(1) "Of Ten Thousand Things There Is not One that does not Worship Way and do Homage to Its 'Power'"

In Lao Zi's thinking, the Way (or Dao) is a metaphysical concept beyond any kind of descriptive language. Just as Lao Zi said, "The Way that can be told

Lao Zi

of is not an Unvarying Way." They contain rich social, political and philosophical thinking such as harmony, justice, appropriateness, order, forgiveness, and modesty. The Way beyond language refers to the abstract and original Way. It represents the origin as well as the comprehensiveness of all things. So it is beyond human language. However, as an ideal political principle of human society, the Way (sometimes "benevolent governance") represents harmony, peace, and justice.

To Lao Zi's mind, Way was a positive value for everybody. It was a treasure for kindhearted people and a protection for evil doers. Lao Zi firmly believed that though the Way was abstract and seemed small and trivial, no one could rule over it. Kings and dukes who seemed powerful and wanted to become rulers of the world had to follow the rules of the Way. If all the kings and dukes followed the rules of the Way, everything in the world would fall into place and be automatically under its rule. Lao Zi even said that if all the kings and dukes followed the rule of the Way, no ghost or evil spirit could disturb them. So in the political philosophical thinking, Lao Zi respected reasoning and disparaged ghosts and spirits.

Lao Zi fully understood that there would be all kinds of conflicts as mankind pursued various interests. He asked people to be good at learning from natural substances and to draw political wisdom from them. He took water as an example when saying, "The highest good is like that of water. The goodness of water is that it benefits the ten thousand creatures; yet itself does not scramble, but is content with the places that all men disdain. It is this that makes water so near to the Way." In praising water so vividly, Lao Zi educated those in power to be good at providing benefits for the people rather than in contending for interest against the people, humbly treating the people and acting like the forgiving seas and rivers. Lao Zi's philosophy was in fact not simply in opposition to the actions of those in power, but he advised those in power to learn from the great saints in history and not be confrontational with the people. Therefore, he reprimanded some of the ministers by saying, ministers who are assisting the king in line with the rules should not force people of the world to become subjects through military power. Wars easily generate bad returns. Thorns thrive in places such as battlefields and it will always be a year of bad omens after a bloody battle.

To Lao Zi, it was a totally erroneous ideology for an intelligent politician to perversely rely on advanced weapons and to feel complacent because of them. The liking of fine weapons, in essence, meant taking killing as a pleasure. Lao Zi had a marvelous elaboration against war: "Weapons are ill-omened things, which the superior man should not depend on. When he has no choice but to use them, the best attitude is to remain tranquil and peaceful. One should never look upon them as things of beauty. For to think them beautiful means to delight in them, and to delight in them means to delight in the slaughter of men. And he who delights in the slaughter of men will never get what he looks for out of those that dwell under heaven."

Lao Zi resolutely opposed war, asked politicians to gently provide people with benefits and to manage the society peacefully. He especially warned politicians that any attempt to carry out their political ideals with military force would doom them to failure. The profound political wisdom of valuing harmony was an ancient political lucidity that today's politicians in all countries should ponder repeatedly.

(a) The issue of justice and fairness in society

Lao Zi often used "benevolent governance" instead of Way. Through praising benevolent governance, he praised social fairness and the fine virtue of non-contention, and he encouraged people to make efforts to achieve benevolence and progress. Through his comparison of heavenly morals and human morals, Lao Zi expressed his desire for social fairness. He said,

"Benevolent governance is like the bending of a bow. When a bow is bent the top comes down and the bottom-end comes up. So too does Heaven take away from those who have too much, and give to those that have not enough. But if it is benevolent governance to take from those who have too much and give to those who have not enough, this is far from being Man's Way. He takes away from those that have not enough in order to make offering to those who already have too much."

Contrary to the fairness of Heavenly Way, human society was "to take away from those that have not enough in order to make offering to those who already have too much." The people were starving as the rulers continued to levy taxes. The people were easily vulnerable to dying because the rulers lived in a debauched way, and their palaces were decorated extravagantly while the farmland was desolate and deserted. He warned the rulers: The greatest threat of danger will come when the people do not respect and fear the threat from the rulers. Do not curse the daily life of the people and do not let people become tired of their lives.

In praising benevolent governance, Lao Zi expressed his desire that rulers should possess the positive virtue of not contending for their own interests against the people. He said, "For it is the way of Heaven not to strive but none the less to conquer, not to speak, but none the less to get an answer, not to beckon, yet things come to it of themselves. Heaven is like one who says little, yet none the less has laid his plans. Heaven's net is wide; coarse are the messes, yet nothing slips through." He hoped that human society would be like the benevolent governance with natural fairness: "Benevolent governance benefits all without harm." Through extolling benevolent governance, he encouraged people to improve themselves for strength and benevolence: "It is benevolent governance, without distinction of persons, to keep the good perpetually supplied."

(b) Ideal society of benevolent governance and a small country with a small population

In Lao Zi's ideal, human society once had its golden age with Great Way prevailing. In that golden time, the people knew there was only one above them ruling society and they felt no pressure from being governed. The politics was that of "benevolent governance," the ideal of the Taoists.

The features of benevolent governance were that a ruler never posed as condescending to the people, and the ruler with virtue would act like saints. He did not mediate social contradictions without principles but cautiously used the symbol of power to levy necessary taxes from the people. When a saint was in power, he would not use the symbol of power to ask for payment of debts. A king with virtue would do as the saint did. Only those without virtue would continue to collect taxes from the people. Lao Zi said that to mediate matters of great resentment without principle would inevitably lead to other resentments and grudges. How could such a ruler administer genuine benevolence?

The social blueprint of "a small country with a small population" best illustrates the ideal of Lao Zi in terms of "benevolent governance." He said, "In a small country with a small population, though there are among the people all kinds of contrivances, they do not use them. They would rather die in their country than migrate. There are boats and carriages, but no one would go in them; there are weapons of war but no one would drill with them. People should have no use for any form of writing save knotted ropes, should be contented with their food, pleased with their clothing, satisfied with their homes, should take pleasure in their rustic tasks. The neighboring country might be so near at hand that one could hear the cocks crowing in it, the dogs barking; but the people would grow old and die without ever having been there."

On the surface, his ideal blueprint for a society seems to be against the progress of civilization, but in fact it expressed his desire for an ideal society where there is no war, no heavy weapons, and people live a peaceful and harmonious life. Except for the "save knotted ropes," "the people would grow old and die without ever having been there," and no one travels in boat or carriage, which are not suitable for modern society, the political ideal for a peaceful and harmonious life in his thinking bears significance for enlightenment.

First, Lao Zi desired small countries with small populations as organizations of human society.

Second, Lao Zi advised people not to have big instruments or utensils, including heavy weapons, not to use advanced means of transportation, and not to show off military power with advanced equipment.

Third, Lao Zi attached great importance to normal tastes, healthy and beautiful clothing, and to satisfaction with the customs.

Fourth, Lao Zi craved a self-sufficient life without one having to travel back and forth and without leaving the family behind in order to make a living. In the *Records of the Historian*, Sima Qian said, "People, jostling back and forth, aim at nothing other than making profits." Lao Zi's wish for no exchanges even till death expressed a kind of sympathy for those who traveled to achieve small profits. Lao Zi's wish and Sima Qian's reading of it were the same, but said in different ways.

(c) A large country must be like the low reaches towards which all streams flow down and act as a womb of the world

Lao Zi, born in the later years of the Spring and Autumn Period, put forth guiding principles for foreign affairs of the various dukedoms under the rule of the Zhou Dynasty in saying: Big dukes should learn from the seas, which are willing to lie low and become the convergent point for all the rivers, much like the wombs of the female animals in various states that lure all the males to woo them. Why is this so? In the animal world, the female with her tranquility often defeats the agitated male. Calmness may preserve modesty. Therefore, big states should treat small states with modesty and they will thus win respect from the small states, while small states will win support from the big states if they treat them with modesty. The purpose of big states' diplomacy is nothing other than to have the small states under them, while that of small states is nothing other than to win support from the big states. Big or small, a state must treat another state with modesty. Particularly, the big states should act modestly. The modest diplomatic tactic bears significance even in today's international community, though it was originally only aimed at the dukes under the Emperor of the Zhou Dynasty. Big countries in today's world should have an honest attitude towards helping the weak and small countries and they will then win their trust. Big countries will not have support from small and weak countries if they attempt to control them.

Lao Zi, in citing the forgiving, modest, and non-contentious sea as an example, urged those dukes of the big states who wanted to acquire the power to rule the world to learn from the sea so as to win the intentions of the people. Human society has its own rules to follow, independent of being manipulated by the intentions of some people. Therefore Lao Zi warned: We believe that he who wants to take over the world and run it according to his own way will not be able to accomplish it. The world is a sacred matter that no one can manipulate by his own will. He who wants to do so will certainly end in failure. He who wants to control it will certainly lose it. Lao Zi reprimanded those in power, saying that they must value virtue and observe the Way. The Way may seem small and trivial, but nothing in the world can rule it. If all the kings and dukes observe the principles of the Way, everything in the world would fall into place automatically. Lao Zi also said, "The Way often looks like it is taking no action, but in fact it can accomplish anything."

(2) "I Have Heard of Letting the World Be and Letting the World Alone, but I Have Never Heard of Governing the World"

Zhuang Zi (369-286 B.C.), who inherited and developed the philosophy of Lao Zi, was just as opposed to wars and, moreover, was opposed to un-principled debates and struggles. He hoped for an ideal society without contradictions and conflicts. In Zhuang Zi's mind, the highest form of peace was peaceful co-existence between people and everything else in nature. The ideal for human society was that it would be without classes, gaps, and differences between nobles and commoners. He wrote a story about the death of Huntun to illustrate his belief.

(a) The death of Huntun
In "Respond to Kings and Emperors" of *Zhuang Zi* (《庄子》), Zhuang Zi wrote the following story: The king of the South Sea State was named Shu and the king of the North Sea State was named Hu. The king of the Central State was named Huntun. One day, King Shu and King Hu came to the Central State. King Huntun treated the two guests with great hospitality. Shu and Hu discussed how they might pay back his friendliness. Everyone knows that human beings have seven apertures (mouth, nostrils, eyes, and ears) in order to eat, breathe, see, and hear. So, they concluded, let us try to chisel seven apertures for him. Therefore, the two of them chiseled one

aperture a day on the body of King Huntun. Seven days later, King Huntun had seven apertures, but he died from this.

What does the death of King Huntun mean? To Zhuang Zi's mind, it meant that there was an artificial undermining of nature. If people want to change nature, or original social customs through their subjective mentality, they will certainly kill nature, destroy original social customs, and finally destroy their own fine intention. Political activities of mankind must respect the order and rule of nature and spontaneous order. Otherwise, mankind will not acquire genuine happiness but will destroy itself.

(b) Horse on the grassland

To Zhuang Zi, a society should not be confined to the likes and dislikes of a ruler, but should be looked after (not managed) according to will of the people and the social customs should be allowed to run their own course. In an ideal society, people should be like a horse on the grassland that grazes when hungry, drinks when thirsty, gallops when excited, and lives freely. This is the true nature of a horse. The high buildings of mankind are of no use for horses on the grassland. Mankind has its own nature. It is natural for human beings to have clothing to wear that is produced through weaving, food to eat that is produced through farming, and everyone should be the same without the differentiation of nobles and commoners.

Zhuang Zi was therefore particularly opposed to rulers who managed state affairs selfishly, and he asked them to follow the example of selfless nature in their political activities while serving the public wholeheartedly. If there is no selfishness and private interest, the social order will be as harmonious as it is in nature, and even the ghosts and spirits will yield to the leadership of selfless rulers.

Zhuang Zi craved for a natural world in which to live and he hoped for a society of more tolerance. He said, "I only know that the ruler should treat the world with a lenient attitude, but I have never heard of manipulating the world according to his own rules." To Zhuang Zi, that would be against the will and instinct of mankind no matter how happy the people might feel under the management of Yao or how painful they might feel under the rule of Zhou. Humans hurt their *Yang* when they were extremely happy and their *Yin* when they became agitated. When humans lost their original internal harmony, society fell into disorder. Therefore, a ruler should let people be indifferent to fame and fortune and keep their harmony. This was the fundamental spirit of no-action politics.

In political ideology, Zhuang Zi was an idealist as well as a romantic. In political reality and practice this is difficult to achieve, but the love and tolerance of his political ideal is something that the great statesmen of this time of globalization should possess. The Way by Zhuang Zi's political ideology contains everything, much like the vast seas. Zhuang Zi described his benevolent governance as containing ten aspects: do not do things intentionally for one's special personal purpose; do not speak intentionally for one's special personal interest; love others and offer benefits for all; treat different people and things with an attitude of equality and tolerance; do not discriminate one against another in daily life; associate with people who have different ideas; adhere to virtue; cultivate every virtue; do things according to the rule of the Way; and do not let other things frustrate the will and aspirations of the people. If one can accomplish the aforementioned, one will bring about the ideal of the benevolent governance.

Zhuang Zi particularly exposed the disasters that were brought about by unfair social practices. He seriously criticized the unjust situation in which "those who steal the knives are executed while those who usurp the states become princes. Now that humaneness and righteousness are observed in the houses of the princes, does it not mean that humaneness, righteousness and sagely wisdom have all been stolen?" He went on further with the appalling conclusion, "As long as the sages do not die, the robbers will not be extinguished." He further demanded the abolition of all artificial rules so as to eradicate all the rules that might cause struggle and contention. Zhuang Zi said, "Therefore, discard the sages and wisdom, and the great robbers will be curbed; destroy the jades and pearls, and the petty robbers will not appear; break the tallies and seals, and the people will be unsophiscated; crush the weights and scales, and the people will no longer quarrel." This radical position on social management of course could not solve social problems, but it reflects Zhuang Zi's wish for an ideal society of justice.

(c) "Animals could be tethered and led about"

In contrast with the ideal society of a small country with a small population put forward by Lao Zi, Zhuang Zi put forth the idea of a society in which people did not struggle against one another, and human beings and everything in nature co-existed peacefully. In such a society, people would move in a leisurely manner, their eyes would be filled with satisfaction instead of looking around in fear. In such a society, there would be no paths in the mountains and no boats on big lakes, villages would be connected with and integrated with each other in lush greeneries. People might even leash animals to play with them. People might peep into the nest of a bird and the bird would not be surprised or shocked. In such a time, there would be no difference between the rich and the poor.

Such an ideal society can neither be found in history nor will it likely be achieved in the far future. Zhuang Zi imagined such a harmonious ideal for humankind to pursue in the hope that it might serve as an ideal resource in the pursuit of peace and harmony between human beings and nature.

Chapter III

The Silk Road and the Economic Ethics of China's Peaceful Development

The Chinese people were the first to cultivate silk moths (*Bombyx mori*) and to use their cocoons to produce natural silk. Ancient Westerners called China Seres or Sinae, the word seres referring to the silk nation. For a considerably long period of time, the Chinese have been experts in the technique of making silk, and the fact that they spread silk-making technology to the Western world has been one of their contributions to world civilization. Over a period of nearly 2,000 years from Zhang Qian, who lived during the Han Dynasty at the end of the second century B.C., up until the 18th century when modern Western industrial civilization began to occupy the world economic and cultural stage, the route of cultural dissemination by way of the "Silk Road" has been a symbol in the process of cultural exchanges between China and the Western countries. Thus the Silk Road represents a kind of economic and cultural ethic in the support of peaceful development. In today's world of economic globalization and cultural diversity, a review of this ancient economic and cultural concept may be of practical significance in the promotion of world peace and the enhancement of happiness for humankind.

1. The Silk Road and the Way for Developing the Economy and Spreading Culture

In the history of economic and cultural exchanges between China and foreign countries, there was a trade passage known as the Silk Road that symbolized a peaceful economy and cultural dissemination. This road, starting east from China, ran through the western regions into ancient India, then Arabia, then Persia, and finally into Greece and ancient Rome. Exchanges over this passageway first started toward the end of the second century B.C. when Zhang Qian of the Han Dynasty pioneered the route leading to the western regions. During the 18th century A.D., the Silk Road as a trade route suddenly came to an end after a history of nearly two thousand years of peaceful economic and cultural exchanges between China and the West. The history of the Silk Road shows that it maintained a most splendid culture for one of the longest periods of trade in human history.

The term "Silk Road," of course, is only the symbol for a series interlinking bonds between the cultures of China and other nations. There was no actual road leading directly to the western regions and the commercial exchanges followed various routes through the mountains and deserts, but many kinds of science and technologies were disseminated over this road and the quantity of silk trade was much smaller than that for other articles.

The person who was the first to name this cultural passageway the "Silk Road" was F. von Richthoften (1833-1905), a German historian and geographer.

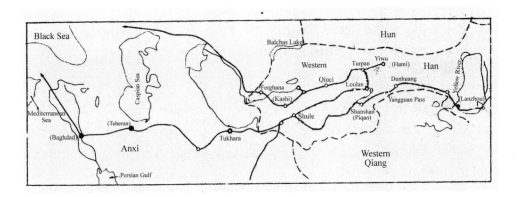

A sketch map illustrating the Silk Road that connected the Eurasia continent

In 1860, he participated in a German economic delegation that visited the Far Eastern Regions including China. After his death, his five-volume book *Notes on a Personal Journey to China and Studies Based on the Journey* (*China: Ergebnesse Eigener Reisen und darauf gegrundeter Studien*, Berlin, 1877-1912) was published. In this great work, he named this commercial passageway, which he said was based mainly on silk trade between China of the Han Dynasty and the southern and western parts of Central Asia as well as India, as the "Silk Road," or "Seidenstrassen" in German. Later, in a book titled *The Ancient Silk Road Between China and Syria*, another German historian named Herman extended the Silk Road to the western banks of the Mediterranean Sea and Asia, and defined the historical and cultural connotations of the "Silk Road" in this way: a land trade communication line running from ancient China to South and West Asia and to Europe and North Africa.

Since on this road a large quantity of good-quality silk fabrics were exported to the Western world, this passageway was figuratively and beautifully called the "Silk Road." The term was gradually acknowledged and put to use throughout international academic circles. Actually, jade, gems, ceramics, lacquer-ware, ironware, and even horses and other articles were also transported by merchants as they traveled on this Silk Road. The music of the Western Region, Indian Buddhism, and the Islamic culture of the Arab world were introduced into China by way of this road. Therefore, we might also call this road a "gemstone road," a "ceramic road," a "Buddhist road," etc.

(1) The Silk Road as Evidence of Peaceful Development in the Economy of the Chinese Nation

After Zhang Qian pioneered the route to the western regions, Chinese culture began to spread continuously into the western regions, West Asia, and other places while the culture of the western regions and West Asia also began to infiltrate into China. This marked the beginning of the time in which Chinese culture and world culture began to influence each other.

Historically, the Silk Road was not a single-line commercial route but rather three main lines. The first line is called the "North Silk Road." It started from Chang'an (now Xi'an) in China and crossed the inland areas of Central Asia to reach the areas of West Asia and the Mediterranean Sea. The second route is called the "Southwest Silk Road." It started from China's city of Chengdu and progressed into Yunnan Province and Burma (Myanmar), reaching India as well as other places of Central Asia. The third route is called the "Silk Road on the Sea." This began on the southwest coast of China, at the port of Nanhai, and crossed the Straits of Malacca to go westwards, arriving at the shores of the Indian Ocean and then reaching as far as some of the countries of North Africa. The first and second Silk Roads had direct relations with the explorer Zhang Qian; although the third Silk Road began in the age of Emperor Wu of the Han Dynasty. It was related mainly to the active explorations made by Ban Chao (32-102), the chief inspector for the Western Han Dynasty. Ban Chao sent out the envoy Gan Ying to Daqin to make contacts with rulers in the West. Although Ban Chao's action was unsuccessful because the envoy was blocked at the Persian Gulf, yet this opened up an historical route for China's cultural exchanges with Europe. The three Silk Roads explored by the Chinese played an active promotional role in cultural dissemination for nearly two thousand years.

Viewed from the angle of economic development, the economic trade over the three roads was basically peaceful, commercial trade without any political compulsiveness, still less the need for escorting the trade caravans with armed forces.

The North Silk Road was explored by Zhang Qian. In 138 B.C., Zhang Qian was sent on a diplomatic mission to the western regions, the first of its kind. On his way he and his companions were captured by a tribe of Huns and forced to live with them for thirteen years. Finally only he and Tang Yifu were left to return alive to the emperor of the Han Dynasty. In 119 B.C., Zhang Qian was sent on a diplomatic mission to the western regions for the second time. The delegation of envoys was huge, carrying with them rich property. They first reached the Osun State, and then deputy envoys with delegations respectively reached the Dawan, Tukhara, Daxia, and other states. After that, the Han Dynasty established formal relations with the various states of the western regions.

The Southwest Silk Road had actually been in existence before the Han Dynasty. When Zhang Qian was sent on the diplomatic mission to the western regions, he reported back to Emperor Wu that he had found another route leading to India and Central Asia. The emperor then planned to unite with Tukhara to launch a pincer military attack on the hostile tribal Hun in order to open up the new passage linking the Han Dynasty with India and Central Asia. However, Emperor Wu failed in this attempt and the Western Han Dynasty could only engage in indirect trading activities with Indian merchants through the medium of various southwest tribes along the Southwest Silk Road. Later, because the people of the Ailao State submitted themselves to the Han Dynasty in 69, the government of the Eastern Han Dynasty began to have direct contacts with the Shan nationality in Burma. After that, the road for commercial and cultural exchanges between China and India progressed in an unimpeded way. Later, Buddhist cultural exchanges between China and India frequently took place by way of this road.

The Silk Road on the Sea was also opened up about the time of Emperor Wu of the Han Dynasty. After he unified southern Guangdong Province in 111 B.C., he sent an envoy to visit various Southeast Asian countries. "The Geographic Notes" of *The History of the Han Dynasty* (《汉书》) gives a record of the time it took to go to various Southeast Asian countries and describes the situations and customs of certain countries there. For example, the customs of Huangzhi State were similar to the customs of Zhuya Prefecture. Other states had expansive lands, large populations, rich variety of things, and also rare and valuable objects for exchanges with the Han Dynasty. In the late years of the Western Han Dynasty, the emperor presented many valuable things to the king of Huangzhi State, and asked for a rhinoceros. There was a Jichengbu State south of Huangzhi State. The official postal courier of the Hans ceased going any further. According to modern research, the Silk Road on the Sea after the reign of Emperor Wu ran from present-day Guangzhou to Viet Nam, Malaysia, and Burma, and then by sailing across the Indian Ocean to the Huangzhi State (Kanchipuram in today's India) in the south of the Indian Peninsula and to Sri Lanka. On this route, despite frequent piratical plunders, the economic activities of the Chinese trading caravans were not accompanied by any acts of military aggression. Therefore, the Silk Road on the Sea was basically a road for peaceful economic and cultural dissemination.

(2) The Silk Road and the Nation's Peaceful Cultural Dissemination

Viewed from the perspective of cultural dissemination, there was never any incident of sanguine heretical slaughter and military subjugation by the Chinese on any of these three roads. In most cases there were just normal official envoys, folk trading caravans, and a small number of monks with lofty cultural ideals traversing these routes from China to the outside world. Those great monks were especially praiseworthy; they overcame unthinkable difficulties and hardships and braved the danger of a slim chance for survival, going to other countries for Buddhist scriptures and promoting and deepening cultural exchanges between China and ancient India.

There were mainly two forms of economic and trading activity on the Silk Road. One was official tributes provided by other states to China and gifts given by the emperor in return; the second was merchants' bartering of goods. Although the various past governments of China, known as a land of propriety, had the political intention of propagating national strength, they handled relations with other countries or nationalities mainly by means of cultural empathy to win over people of these countries and not by military subjugation.

The traditional Confucian "theory of benevolence and virtue" had a profound influence on the diplomatic and political work of ancient China. The Chinese governments in powerful and prosperous periods attracted those on the other side to submit to them mostly by way of presenting them with exquisite things. Along the ancient Silk Road, a considerable amount of goods were gifts that were given to other governments by the Chinese emperors and tributes provided in return by the various governments. Particularly during the period of "making peace with other nationalities" the articles granted by the Chinese government to minority ethnic groups were all in the form of peaceful economic exchanges. This kind of official activity designed for friendly contacts, to a very great extent, stipulated that economic activities on the Silk Road were peaceful economic and trading activities. When he was sent on a diplomatic mission to the western regions for the second time, Zhang Qian brought with him a huge sum of money to unite the Han Dynasty with the Osun State and other countries of the western regions.

During the time of Emperor Taizong of the Tang Dynasty (618-907), when Princess Wencheng entered Tibet, she brought with her not only a large quantity of silk fabric and other articles, but also a large number of men of letters and scientific and technological personnel. The dowry Emperor Taizong provided for her included a Buddhist image of Sakyamuni, the founder of Buddhism; various kinds of jewelry, gold, and jade ornaments; 360 volumes of classical books, 300 titles of classical divination books, 60 kinds of technical books, 100 kinds of prescriptions, four medical works, five kinds of diagnosis, and six kinds of medical apparatus. She also brought cereal and turnip seeds with her, and even some cooked foods, brocade cushions and blankets of various floral designs, as well as things for discerning good from bad. Thereafter, cultural exchanges between the Tang Dynasty and the Tibetan regime allowed this Tibetan regime to become the most powerful and prosperous country on the western border of China at that time.

Zheng He of the Ming Dynasty made seven oceanic voyages, bringing with him articles from the government of the Ming Dynasty and thus forging profound friendships with Southeast Asian countries. As regards the Chinese and Western caravans active along the Silk Road, most of them were composed of profit-making merchants engaging mainly in economic and trading activities and supplying each other's needs without political and religious aims.

Some Chinese monks who went to India for Buddhist scriptures were most praiseworthy. Supported by their highly pious religious beliefs, they overcame all sorts of difficulties and hardships hardly bearable to ordinary people, and gained from India numerous classical Buddhist books, thus deepening the cultural exchanges between China and India. The monk Xuan Zang, who went to study Buddhism in India, greatly promoted political and cultural exchanges between Emperor Taizong of the Tang Dynasty and Rajaputra Siladiya (590-647) of Central India. The great emperor and great king sent friendly envoys to each other, granted each other gifts, and thus enhanced friendship between the peoples of China and India.

Through the Silk Road, China's ironware, lacquer-ware, and the four inventions of ancient China — paper, printing, gun powder, and compass — spread one after another to Western Asia and Europe. In the meantime, the western regions' music, India's Buddhism, and Europe's Christianity were introduced into China. Therefore, it can be said without any exaggeration that the ancient Silk Road was a road for peaceful dissemination of culture and civilization.

2. Profit Established Through Righteousness

The "distinction between righteousness and profit" has been an important ideological concept in traditional Chinese culture. Scholars generally incorporate this question into the scope of research on Chinese ethics. As a matter of fact, this ethics issue in relationship to today's international community can be extended to economic matters concerning how the Chinese handle international relations.

The connotations of the "distinction between righteousness and profit" can roughly be divided into the viewpoints of three different schools of Chinese philosophy. The viewpoint of the first school sets righteousness against profit, advocating the priority of righteousness and valuing righteousness to the neglect of profit. Its representatives are Confucius, Mencius, Zeng Zi (the author of the *Great Learning*), Dong Zhongshu, Cheng Hao, Cheng Yi, and Zhu Xi. The second school of thought stresses profit but does not exclude righteousness. This school of thought stands for the integration of righteousness with profit, and takes social utility as the goal. Representatives of this school are the pre-Qin Mozi and his disciples, and Yan Fu and Liang Qichao of modern China. The third school of thought gives consideration to both righteousness and profit. In the first school of thought there were people who advocated "controlling profits through righteousness," such as the pre-Qin Xun Zi; Li Gou, Chen Liang, and Ye Shi of the Song Dynasty; Wang Fuzhi and the Yan-Li (Yan Yuan and Li Gong) school of thought of the Qing Dynasty. Some of these advocated that legitimate profit is righteousness, such as thinker Li Zhi of the late Ming Dynasty. But in China's cultural tradition, the Confucian thinking represented by Confucius, Mencius, Dong Zhongshu, and Zhu Xi has always held the dominant position. Therefore, the concept of "establishing profit through righteousness," "generating profit with righteousness," and "controlling profit with righteousness" has deeply affected the Chinese people's view of righteousness and profits so that, in handling the relationship between the two, the Chinese are used to considering the legality of benefits from the angle of morality. This mode of thinking affects the Chinese policy-makers.

Of course, the emphasis on the priority of righteousness over profit doesn't mean denying profits. Rather, it only stresses the fact that pursuit of benefits must be predicated and based on a proper morality. Only profits pursued in accordance with morality and righteousness can be long-lasting and reliable. Otherwise, the acquisition of profit can only be temporary and not positive. The Chinese do not deny the pursuit of legitimate profits, but combine the pursuit of legitimate profits with the principle of justice, holding that the pursuit of legitimate profits itself is righteous. These thoughts encourage the Chinese to actively participate in the world economic competition and also encourage them to consider rightful principles in their contacts with various nations around the world. Thus they are providing their own theoretical resources for the establishment of an international order under the new international situation.

(1) The Righteousness-Profit Concept in the Pre-Confucius Age

The two words "righteousness" and "profit" appeared quite early in ancient Chinese writings, in the *Remarks of Monarchs* by Zuo Qiuming that recorded the statements of aristocrats at the end of Western Zhou Dynasty, and in the *Zuo Zhuan* where some statesmen began to mention righteousness and profit together thus gradually raising this issue to a philosophical level. The *Zuo Zhuan* says: While expounding necessary preconditions for victory in war, Shen Shushi of the Chu State put forward the concept of righteousness and profit as "establishing profit through righteousness." In the *Remarks of Monarchs*, an unnamed statesman set forth the idea that "satisfaction with profit means righteousness."

It can be said that only in Confucianism does the righteousness and profit issue really become a matter concerning the relationship between morality and economy. Therefore it involves the relationship between social utility and social justice (the aspect of morality), and the relationship between personal moral behavior and the acquisition of personal profits.

In "Zhou Yu" of the *Remarks of Monarchs*, some enlightened literati and officialdom openly opposed the king's "special profit," that is, monopoly of interests. For example, Rui Liangfu, in the age of King Li of the Western Zhou Dynasty, opposed Rong Yigong, a favorite minister of King Li, on the grounds that Rong Yigong was keen on "special profit" while exploiting the people by taking away their profits, and he would therefore soon meet with a disastrous calamity. In Rong's opinion, profits were generated by all things on earth and so should be commonly possessed by the world. He argued that if profits were monopolized by one person, this would cause great harm. A true king, he said, should distribute profits to people in all strata, so that the gods, people, and all things would be in a balanced state. King Li didn't accept Rui's advice, and so Rui was later exiled to the distant Shanhaiguan Pass.

In the 13th year of the rule of King Xiang (638 B.C.) of the Eastern Zhou Dynasty, the State of Zheng prepared to send a punitive expedition against the State of Hua. King Xiang sent an envoy to the State of Hua to mediate the dispute. The State of Zheng seized the envoy sent by King Xiang. Enraged by this, the king decided to use the armed forces of the Di Nationality to suppress the State of Zheng. A senior official named Fu Chen advised King Xiang that the contradictions between Zhou and the State of Zheng were disagreements between brothers, and so the king should not invite forces from outside to interfere. The Di people were outsiders, and inviting them to assist meant sending what was good to others. At the same time, it would show everyone that we had enmity with our brothers. This would be an unjust act. "What is righteousness used for?" he asked. "Righteousness is used to generate profits. When an action is not in conformity with the requirement of righteousness, the profit gained can't be rich." But King Xiang finally didn't accept the advice of the official Fu Chen, insisting on using the forces of Di people to suppress the State of Zheng. This led to an attack by the Di people against King Xiang. Finally it was Jin Wengong (king of the State of Jin) who repulsed the Di people and safeguarded the dignity of King Xiang.

During the reign of King Xiangong (?-651 B.C.) of the State of Jin, disputes occurred among the dukes and princes over the question of who should be the successor to the throne. The ministers of the Jin court also had different opinions as to this matter. Some ministers, taking a stand for safeguarding the position of imperial power, said that the successor, be he the eldest son or the second son, would be legal as long as he was so designated by King Xiangong. Other ministers, who were in charge of the ceremonial and musical system, opposed this insisting that one must follow the principle of righteousness in serving the king. For example, Zheng Pi said, "I know of the principle of waiting upon the king, complying with the requirement of righteousness, but not currying favor with the king when his understanding is erroneous. The reason people need the leadership of the king is because of the need to embody the governance rules of righteousness. Righteousness is used to generate profit, while profit is used to bring affluence to the people."

King Xiangong's subsequent breaking of the tradition of passing the throne of dukes and princes to the eldest son of his legal wife under the ceremonial and musical system of the Zhou Dynasty led to internal political confusion. Three senior officials separated into three opposing forces. One of these, Zheng Pi was prepared to accept the political and military forces of the Di people and the State of Qin to launch a palace coup and support the promotion of the crown prince, Shensheng, to the throne. Another official, Li Ke, then stepped forward to say that he negated Zheng Pi's line of action. He said, "The righteousness we talk about is the foundation on which profit stands. Greed is the base on which grudges are generated. When righteousness is abolished, profit cannot stand; excessive greediness makes the generation of grudges possible."

Under the ceremonial and musical system established during the Zhou Dynasty, great attention was paid to the priority of social justice. This ideological tradition was passed from generation to generation by various officials. In the book *Zuo Zhuan*, it is recorded that some important statesmen, proceeding from the spirit of the ceremonial and musical system, were often able to persuade the king in regard to his behavior. The book further records that the State of Zheng, in the face of threats from the State of Jin, requested the State of Chu to provide it with political and military protection. Answering the request of the State of Zheng, the State of Chu decided to send troops to aid the State of Zheng. When the troops passed by the residence of Shen Shushi, the high official Da Si Ma made it a point to meet with Shen and ask him to predict the outcome of the dispatching of troops. Shen expounded conditions for war from a high political plane. He said the six conditions for launching a war are: virtue, punishment, auspiciousness, justice, sense of propriety, and faith. Virtue is used to bring benefits to the people; punishment is used to support justice and get rid of evil; auspiciousness is used to comply with the ghosts and gods; justice is used to establish social utility; the sense of propriety is used to befit all occasions; and faith is used to keep all things in existence. When the people live an affluent life and have a correct morality, everything will be beneficial to the people and the country. Furthermore, if the action taken is appropriate and in conformity with climatic conditions and everything is crowned with success, the state will be in harmony from top to bottom. All moves, all actions taken should be gentle, everything should be prepared for what one wants to seek, and everybody should know the norms. Only when a war is launched under these conditions will it be possible to win a victory. Now diplomatically, the State of Chu abandoned its previous allies, while in regard to its international affairs, it waged the war precisely during spring plowing season when the people were toiling exceedingly hard. Chu would be sure to lose. The result was that the war ended with the defeat of the State of Chu.

In this famous dialog given during the discussion on war conditions, Shen Shushi analyzed the relations between righteousness and profit from the angle of a statesman. He regarded righteousness as the value of a tool, and treated profit as the value of a goal. This viewpoint is somewhat different from the subsequent Confucian understanding of the relations between righteousness and profit. But at least Shen Shushi saw the foundation for the establishment of social utility — the social role of righteousness. Therefore, in China's mainstream ideological tradition, the positive role of righteousness has always received the highest attention. The question about the "distinction between righteousness and profit" was later discussed further in Confucian ideology.

(2) The "Righteousness-Profit View" of Confucius

(a) "A gentleman takes as much trouble to discover what is righteousness as lesser men take to discover what profit they can make."

Confucius was the thinker who was first to systematically expound on the issue of righteousness and profit, and he stressed righteousness to the neglect of profit. The reason he stressed righteousness and despised profit is closely related to his philosophical ideals in terms of education. He intended to only train gentlemen with noble character, and not ordinary scholars. Therefore, one cannot make simplified explanations about Confucius' thinking in stressing righteousness to the neglect of profit. One of his disciples said, "Confucius seldom talks about profit," adding that Confucius says that acting upon the requirement of profit is bound to generate more grudges.

Confucius made a relatively comprehensive exposition on "gentleman," saying that a gentleman takes the cultivation of character as fundamental, and regulates his behavior in compliance with the requirement of etiquette; makes friends with a modest attitude, and builds up his character with honesty and credibility. That is a gentleman. In Confucius' eye, a gentleman is a perfect man, an "accomplished man" — the final perfection of character. In Confucius' opinion, as long as a person thinks about whether he should get something or not when he sees a profit, whether he dares to sacrifice his life at a time of danger, and despite spending days of longtime difficulties and hardships, he doesn't forget his promises made in ordinary times, then it can be said that he is a perfect man.

Then, how is one to distinguish between a gentleman and a lesser person? In Confucius' eye, the essential distinction between a gentleman and a lesser person lies in whether he takes righteousness as the goal of his life, or takes profit as the goal of his life. Precisely because of this, although a gentleman also advocates bravery, he must take righteousness as the highest standard. Otherwise he is no different from a robber. So Confucius said that a gentleman's bravery is expressed in what he should do in terms of morality and justice, which is therefore helpful to the stability of social order; a lesser man's bravery is prompted by profit, and he therefore may become a robber and endanger the tranquility of the social order.

In order to give prominence to the responsibility to be undertaken by a gentleman, Confucius even said, "Coming out to serve as an official, a gentleman aims entirely at propagating righteousness. I have long been aware that general principles are no longer practicable." What Confucius expressed here is a pure idealistic attitude toward life and the sentiment of saving the world.

Although Confucius' "righteousness-profit concept" sets a strict demand on a gentleman's morality, he didn't simply negate a gentleman's pursuit of legitimate benefits, especially ordinary people's act of pursuing interests. If the profit gained is legitimate, then it is fine to be a cart driver to get it. Politically, Confucius paid special attention to administrators bringing benefits to the people and he "opposed rulers competing with the people for profits." This idea was brought further into full play by Mencius.

(b) "If those above and those below strive to snatch profit one from the other, the state will be endangered."

Mencius lived in the middle of the Warring States Period, which was an age of mutual competition by force among princes. In their wars for supremacy, some princes gained advantageous positions and devoted themselves heart and soul to economic development, while relatively neglecting the problem of social justice and ethics and morality

Within the states of the princes, Mencius, as the spokesman for the conscience of the time, followed the example of Confucius. He remained busy running among the various states of princes, trying hard to publicize the ideals of Confucian benevolence and righteousness. Once in an eloquent dialog with King Hui of the State of Liang, Mencius cleverly criticized his thinking. Mencius explicitly revealed the danger King Hui might encounter in his wholehearted pursuit of profits. When King Hui said to him, "Venerable sir, since you have made light of the distance of a thousand *li*, you may have some way to profit my state, mayn't you?" Mencius promptly answered, "Why should Your Majesty have mentioned the word 'profit'? What counts is benevolence and righteousness. If Your Majesty says, 'How can I profit my state?' the high officials will say, 'How can we profit our fiefs?' and the intellectuals and the commoners will say, 'How can we profit ourselves?' If those above and those below strive to snatch profit one from the other, the state will be endangered.... But if profit comes first and righteousness second, the killers will not be satisfied without seizing possession of whatever they covet. No benevolent man ever neglects his parents, and no righteous man ever looks down upon his sovereign. Your Majesty should talk about only benevolence and righteousness, but why should you have mentioned the word 'profit'?"

On another occasion, Mencius asked Song Keng, another public figure lobbying the prince, where he was going. Song Keng said that he recently heard that the State of Chu was going to make war on the State of Qin, so he was going to see the King of Chu in order to persuade him not to send troops. The State of Chu was not happy after they learned of his intention. Song Keng was also prepared to see the King of Qin in order to dissuade him from dispatching troops. Mencius asked Song Keng, "For what reason are you trying to stop the State of Qin from sending troops?" Song answered, "I wish to explain in detail the disadvantages of their dispatching troops." Hearing this, Mencius found Song's lobbying view to be problematic. He told Song bluntly, "Your intention of dissuading the King of Qin from sending troops is commendable, but it is not practical to explain the matter merely from the angle of disadvantages. Since you are persuading the two kings of Qin and Chu from the angle of utility, requiring them to stop sending troops out of consideration for profit, the soldiers of the armed services who are happy about not going to war will also take delight in utility. If the subjects of a state wait on their king only out of consideration for their own profits, and children attend to their parents with the mindset of utility, and people as brothers treat their elder brothers also only with the mindset of utility, the result is bound to be a departure from the ethical rule of benevolence and morality between king and minister, between father and son, and between elder and younger brothers."

In the above-mentioned two passages of famous dialogs, Mencius gave prominence to the contradiction between righteousness and profit in an exceedingly clear-cut manner, holding that the highest ruler of a state should be concerned with the legitimacy and rationality of the social moral principle and should not directly pursue profits. Direct pursuit of profits will mislead people so that they run after profits heart and soul and thus lose any concern about justice. The result will put the king of a state in political crisis. Therefore, Mencius firmly maintained that in exercising administration, a state must take benevolence and righteousness as the highest principle. Otherwise, the state will inevitably head for destruction.

Similar to this viewpoint of Mencius, the author of the *Great Learning* held that a country should not directly pursue profits, but should take justice as profit. The author maintained that a state does not regard actual material benefit as its own advantage; rather, it regards moral righteousness as its own profit. If someone holds the political power of a state and he wholeheartedly pursues profits, that would be the practice of a lesser man. Political power of a state held in the hand of a lesser man is bound to cause the arrival of both disaster and scourge. At this time, even if there are some kind-hearted people in the state, they can do nothing about the matter!

This kind of viewpoint and proposition means that a state should not regard actual material benefits as its own benefits, and here lies the principle that it should take moral righteousness as its benefit. We needn't bother about whether a king can act as required by Confucianism in political activity. The thinking of some pre-Qin Confucians who put a special emphasis on the priority of morality and on maintaining moral action in the pursuit of profits in the activity of a state has exerted an extremely profound influence on some subsequent Confucian scholars, such as Dong Zhongshu of the Western Han Dynasty, the two brothers Cheng Hao and Cheng Yi of the Northern Song Dynasty, and Zhu Xi of the Southern Song Dynasty. All of them are representatives of this kind of ideology and concept. It can be said that the Confucian "righteousness-profit concept" spares no effort to demand putting moral righteousness in the supreme position. This kind of outlook holds a prevailing position in traditional Chinese ideology and actual political life.

(3) "Profit Means the Harmony of Righteousness"

In regard to righteousness and the relationship between righteousness and profit, the authors of the present edition of *The Selected Works on Changes* and the silk edition of *The Selected Works on Changes* had different views. The author of the present edition maintains that righteousness is an external standard used specially to prohibit people from doing illegitimate things. However, in the view of the author of the silk edition, righteousness is an external behavior standard used to enable people to get benefits. These two ways of understanding of righteousness actually define the social role of righteousness from different angles. It can be said that the present edition defines the social role of righteousness from the angle of passive prevention, while the silk edition defines the connotation of righteousness from a positive angle.

In *The Selected Works on Changes*, the author defines the meaning of righteousness from the point of view of the relationship between righteousness and profit. However, in the opinion of the author of the silk edition *Selected Works on Changes*, profit is a harmony of various social norms (righteousness) and to keep them from mutual conflict. If a ruler's behavior suffices to make all things gain their own benefit, then harmony can be reached among various kinds of social norms. The author assumed the tone of advising a ruler, affirming the complementary relationship between legitimate profit and the legitimacy of social norms. This view did not strongly emphasize the absolute priority of righteousness, as does Confucianism.

Yet the issue is how to keep the social legitimacy and suitability. The author presented his own views about this, saying in effect: In knowing the goal and striving to realize it, it is permissible to discuss with such a person the prediction for the development of things. He then will know the estimated time for terminating the process and can put an end to it in time. It is alright to discuss the matter with such a person so as to keep the development of things in a suitable state. Therefore, righteousness is closely associated with the environment surrounding things. This is precisely the spirit of "suiting things to a changed situation," consistently stressed by "philosophy of changes."

It is also said in *The Selected Works on Changes*, "On the earth, straight is used to explain correct character, and square is used to explain suitable conduct. A gentleman should take the earth as an example, and keep his heart upright with an attitude of utter respect. He should set external things right through suitability of conduct so as to ensure that he has a respectful heart and appropriate behavior. Thus he can widely spread virtue and will not sink into an isolated and helpless state." It can thus be seen that to unite people, one must take rightfulness of behavior as the prerequisite. Although the "philosophy of changes" emphasizes change in regard to social unity and social management, it pays great attention to the value of legitimate social regulation per se. This is the great difference between the "philosophy of changes" and Taoist philosophy.

110

3. "Extended Love and Shared Profit"

The Mohist concept of "extended love" was once censured as fatherless ethics by Mencius on the grounds that Mohism fails to differentiate love of one's own father from the love of others' fathers, thus violating the basic principles of "benevolent love of others" and "parents are great," which are consistently upheld in Confucianism. Mencius' criticism of the Mohist ethical ideology can be looked upon as dispute between different schools of thought and should not be regarded as a criterion for judging the value of Mohism. Speaking from the angle of the general ethics needed by modern society, Mohist economic thought as expressed in the words "extended love and shared profit" can provide valuable ideological resources for the establishment of modern economic ethics by Chinese society today, after going through a modern re-explanation.

In the early Warring States period, Mo Zi, the creator of the Mohist school, stopped the State of Chu from invading the State of Song through debate. The picture is a copy of the *Mo Zi* printed in blue with movable bronze type in Zhicheng, Fujian in 1552.

(1) The World Lives with Righteousness, and Dies Without Righteousness

Among the pre-Qin Dynasty thinkers, Mohism was a school of thought that inherited Confucianism and at the same time pushed Confucianism in a new direction. The righteousness-profit view that the Mohists advocated was basically an altruist concept of utility that takes the welfare of thousands of people in society as its goal. However, this altruist concept of utility did not insistently emphasize utility to the neglect of the legitimacy of morality. On the contrary, the Mohists paid great attention to the legitimacy and priority of morality. For example, the Mohists said, "Nothing is more valuable than righteousness."

In order to promote his social ethics (righteousness), Mo Zi (c. 479-381 B.C.) spared no effort in campaigning everywhere. One day he went from the State of Lu to the State of Qi. When he passed by the residence of a good friend, the friend said to him: "The people of the world do not observe righteousness, so what is the need for you to so painstakingly promote righteousness?" Mo Zi replied, "Take a family for example. The family has ten sons, but only one cultivates the land, and the remaining nine do not. Then, shouldn't this son redouble his efforts to till the land? Why should he do so? Because more people eat, while fewer people do farm work! Precisely in today's world most people do not abide by righteousness, so you should advise me to strive to promote righteousness and you should not try to stop my actions!" It is clear from this passage in the dialog that Mo Zi did not promote his principle of righteousness — the legitimacy of morality — in a way that is different from what modern Western society understands as the "justice" principle. Instead, he understood the importance of pressing forward with righteousness from the angle of a utility needed by society. Therefore, we can call it an altruist concept of righteousness and profit.

In the eyes of Mo Zi, righteousness was important because the principle of righteousness was beneficial to all the people of society. He said, "We treasure valuable things because they are beneficial to the people. Righteousness is the thing that can bring people benefit, so we say that righteousness is a good and valuable thing in the world." Proceeding precisely from the angle of social utility, Mo Zi specifically emphasized the social role of righteousness. He said, "People of the world who possess the principle of righteousness can live and without this principle they will die; with the principle of righteousness, they will advance toward affluence, without this principle they will head toward poverty; with the principle of righteousness they will move to order, without this principle they will head for chaos." Since righteousness was so important to human society, Mo Zi further raised the sacredness of righteousness to an extraordinary position, and regarded righteousness as a heavenly demand on the supreme ruler – the emperor. It is precisely because heaven demands that the emperor uncondi- tionally love ordinary people and work for their benefit that the implemen- tation of righteousness in the world has the significance of absolute order. Therefore, the Mohist stress of righteousness has a religious and ideological origin. This is the unique characteristic of the early-stage Mohist "right- eousness-profit concept."

Viewed as a comparison between the two philosophies, the righteous- ness referred to by Mo Zi and his understanding of the relationship between righteousness and profit are quite different from that of Confucianism. The righteousness described by Mo Zi includes a two-faceted content: First, righteousness means non-aggression toward the fruits of the labor of others and other countries. In Mo Zi's opinion, attacking the country of others and robbing others' property is "what is called unjustness." Second, benefiting others is called righteousness. Mo Zi advocated that a person of strength should help others as quickly as possible; a propertied person should give part of his property to others; and a person of high intelligence should teach others patiently. Viewed from the above two points, the righteousness re- ferred to by Mohism is different from the righteousness mentioned by Con- fucianism in terms of propriety. Confucianism specially emphasizes that people of different classes and people playing different social roles under the system of propriety should gain their due and accomplish what they should. The basic condition of the righteousness referred to by Mo Zi is one of not impairing others' interests and it sets a high demand on helping others. Thus it is a kind of utilitarianism carrying the altruist color.

The profit referred to by Mohism was the profit of ordinary people, and therefore the profit he pursued was that of the public interest of the world's people. Mo Zi said, "The morality of the emperor is the great benefit of the world," and that is what it means. Proceeding from the standard of making everything benefit the public, Mo Zi set this as a criterion for the judgment of all actions in ancient society: "All activities can be stopped as long as they are sufficient to provide for people's daily necessities. The action of engaging in various kinds of extra consumption that cannot add benefit to the people shouldn't be done by the emperor." There is, of course, a theo- retical loophole in this saying of Mo Zi. Because people of different times have different demands for profit, and some people's demands are not necessarily reasonable, it is a difficult matter to set any criterion for determining whether a thing or action is beneficial to the people. But the saying of Mo Zi contains the ethics of a thrifty, plain, and simple life, and this kind of ethics invariably has the tendency of helping to protect ecological resources. The Mohist idea of encouraging simple funeral ceremonies and simple living standards is also conducive to protecting ecological resources.

After Mo Zi's death, later Mohists inherited and developed Mo Zi's concept of righteousness and profit. *The Mohist Classics* (《墨经》) says, Righteousness can bring benefit to the world. The book *On Classics* 《经说》) further explains: Righteousness that is aimed for the good of the world's people can bring benefits to the world, but it will not necessarily exert a direct role in each specific matter. Furthermore, on the question of how to get profits, it sets forth the utilitarian concept of taking the largest from among the possible kinds of profit and the smallest from among the possible harms. Clearly, the later Mohists mainly laid their theoretical emphasis on the positive role exerted by the principle of righteousness in the overall interests of society. They also saw that in the process of concrete implementation, righteousness does not necessarily bring direct benefits to each person and in every specific matter.

The later Mohists provided further expositions on the choice of profit, embodying an enhancement in the people's ability of rational judgment in regard to righteousness and profit. For example, the article "Taking the Lion Share" in *The Mohist Classics* says: The result of a person's choice of chopping off a finger and preserving the palm is an expression of the choice of taking a bigger interest from among various profits and taking a smaller harm from among various harms. But this is not actually choosing harm, it is choosing a profit because the choice made under such circumstances is a choice made in a helpless state under others' control. For example, a person assaulted by a robber agrees to let his finger be cut off in order to preserve his whole body. This is an act of achieving a profit. However, the matter of his meeting the robber is itself a kind of harm. Choosing a bigger interest from among various profits is not an act taken against one's will, while choosing a smaller harm from among various harms is an act taken without other alternatives. Getting something under a circumstance wherein it was originally non-existent is an action of choosing a bigger interest from among the general profits. Choosing to give up a certain kind of thing that originally belongs to oneself is an act of choosing a smaller harm from among a variety of harms. An ethical rule means increasing what can be increased and reducing what can be reduced in accordance with the principle of righteousness.

The profit mentioned by both the early-stage and later-stage Mohists referred to the interests of the broad masses of people. In his article "Be Thrifty in Use," Mo Zi put forward this proposal: Productive activity can be stopped as long as people's daily needs are satisfied, actions that cause various kinds of consumption but cannot bring benefits to the people are things that should not be done by the emperor. This utilitarian thinking that takes the public's interests as the fundamental interest has something of a linkage with the utilitarianism of modern Western philosophy, the ideology that encourages working for the greatest happiness for the overwhelming majority of the people.

(2) "Extended Love, Shared Profit"

In the ranks of the ancient thinkers of the pre-Qin Dynasty, the economic principle put forward by Mo Zi, as contained in his words "extended love and shared profit," was an outlook that still has great vitality. Even though this ancient ethical principle, born more than 2,000 years ago, cannot be mechanically copied for use in handling international relations today, it may still provide a useful path toward world peace if adjusted to modern conditions.

(a) "Extended love" used in handling international relations and its interpretation in modern times

Mo Zi's idea of "extended love and shared profit" dealt specifically with the disputes among the dukes and princes in the early Warring States Period. A prince's state at that time did not have the same element of power as one of today's sovereign states may have. Its "extended love" ethics, however, was a matter of exploring both inter-personal relationships and exchanges among different social organizations. Its form can be said to have something of use for today's international ethics. In the eyes of Mo Zi, in order to achieve the aim of peaceful exchange among human groups, one must follow a basic prerequisite, that is, to look upon the other groups as one looks upon one's own group. Both are "self-love" and "self-benefit" groups. Since neither group will do things that harm its own group, people should step out of the confines of "self-love" and "self-benefit" and take the attitude of "examining my group" to treat the "other group" in the form of an analogy, handling contradictions between "my group" and the "other group" by way of comparing the hearts of each.

Although the Mohist concept of "extended love" belongs to an ideological system different from Christianity's "universal love," there are things between the two that can be seen to be similar.

It should be admitted that whether it is the Mohist "extended love" ethics or the theory of rights under the modern "international law" system, both outlooks are based on a theory of selfishness. But in comparison, the theory of "right" has the tendency of inducing and aggravating a psychological gulf between my group and another group. Under the guidance of the theory of "right," various nations and countries may further intensify their psychology of "guarding" themselves against others. In a given historical stage, each nation has to enhance its own military strength to protect its own "rights" from infringement. As to how to break through the limitations of the theory of "right," it is a matter of vital importance for humankind to develop another mode of thinking about the matter of handling relations between "my group" and the "others' group" and between nations, thereby laying a new social foundation.

Viewed from a basic starting point, the German philosopher Kant (1724-1804) and Mo Zi were in agreement in finding that there was a fundamental reason for realizing human beings' peaceful coexistence. Their differences lay in the fact that Kant found this to be the theory of "right," while Mo Zi found it to be the ethics of "extended love" and "shared benefit." Historically, Kant's "right" theory laid down a philosophical foundation for today's international order, but it also had its own shortcomings in that this "right" theory often leads to a kind of "guarding" psychology, and under the influence of this psychology it is impossible for humankind to eliminate the root cause of war. Modern international society must achieve another kind of thinking if it is to correct the defects in this "right" theory. One of the ideological resources to do this is the Mohist ethics on group contacts as expressed in the words "extended love and shared benefit." Although this ethics of group contacts didn't and couldn't relate to international ethics at the time, it has remained a matter of personal ethics and political ethics, and it is entirely possible for us to follow the Mohist train of thought in making a reasonable and logical transformation of this ethics into the international sphere so that it suits the needs of today's and the future international community.

In parts 1, 2, and 3 of "Extended Love," Mo Zi cited two incidents in trying to prove the feasibility of the "extended love" principle. One assumed that there were two officials, the first who championed the ethical principle of "extension" and the second who promoted the ethical principle of "another." Mo Zi asked the question, when people are in difficulty, do they seek help from the first official advocating "extension" or from the second official advocating the ethical principle of "another?" Mo Zi said that people would certainly choose the "official advocating extension" because he would treat his friend in the same way that he treated himself; and would treat a relative of his friend as he would his own relative. This official's attitude toward his friend would be like this: "He feeds his friend when he is hungry; clothes him when he feels cold; nurses him when he is sick, and buries him when he dies." While the "official advocating another" would turn a blind eye to his friend in difficulty. In that case, how could people choose him?

In the second instance he assumed two monarchs, one holding to "extension" and the other holding to the principle of "another." Mo Zi again asked the reader: Would you want to be subject of the monarch "holding to extension" or subject of the monarch "holding to another?" Mo Zi believed people would definitely wish to be subjects of the "monarch holding to extension" because such a monarch would definitely put thousands of people "before himself," then "he steps back to have a look at thousands of people, he feeds them when they are hungry; clothes them when they feel cold; nurses them when they are sick and buries them when they die." Clearly, as an ethical principle for the international community today and for a considerably long period of time to come, "extended love" is an actual possibility. Our human society needs such an ethical principle as the foundation by which to standardize the behavior of various nations and countries.

Of course, the international community of today is more complicated than the agricultural society of the past. A country "holding to extension" can neither go all out to help another country nor help all countries in temporary difficulty. There is the problem of actual capability here. Furthermore, the ethical principle of "extended love and shared benefit" that we are discussing is not merely a question of mutual assistance. It is, first of all, a question of the basic psychological starting point for international contacts. In other words, does each international action that we take in treating other nations and countries grow out of a mindset of concern and openness? In terms of the present international community, the developed countries of the first and second world should not view other nations and countries as "not being of the same clan as mine." Also they should not purposefully set up checks to the economy and trade and should not shift polluting industries to developing countries. Instead, they should, with a basic view toward the integration of humankind, genuinely transform various polluting industries.

A "commercial spirit" has long united various nations around the world in a common market, and many problems of human society have quickly become international problems such as Aids, drug-taking, and drug-trafficking. These problems cannot be resolved by just a "right" theory. They require humankind to embrace a new kind of intercourse ethics, "extended love." Human beings should continue to exist, satisfy their own needs to the maximum, and achieve the essence of their own freedom. To this end, they must take "extended love" as the ethics of international contact, and in an open mind of "love" they should transcend the guarding psychology of the "right" ethics, thereby actually realizing the human's overall utility goal of "shared benefits."

(b) The international ethics of "extended love and shared benefit" and the ideal state of humankind

A specific case can shed light on the necessity of "shared benefits." For the General Motors Corperation, in the case of every US $10,000 paid for goods, $3,000 belongs to South Korean assembly workers, $1,750 to the Japanese parts and components manufacturing firms, $750 to the German designing engineers, $400 to the parts-making merchants of Taiwan, Singapore, and other places, and $250 to the sales-promoting service of British advertisement companies. The remaining money of less than $4,000 is given to the car engineers of Detroit, to the lawyers and banks of New York, to Washington's lobby-men, to the insurance companies of America and to the shareholders of the General Motors. This indicates that in economic globalization, reciprocity and mutual benefit is a practical issue, and not merely a theoretical one. International ethics that reflects the present international relationships must be established on the basis of this fact. We cannot remain in an age when there is only "international law" without international ethics.

As a matter of fact, Kant once predicted that the commercial spirit would sooner or later control every nation. This commercial spirit is bringing various sovereign states together through the behavior of each other's desire for profits, thereby forcing various countries to promote peace, and after any outbreak of war, to take advantage of this kind of "each other's self-profit" to mediate contradictions and prevent war. In the *Communist Manifesto*, Karl Marx and Friedrich Engels expounded in detail the contents of global economic integration. They said: "The bourgeoisie has, through its exploitation of the world market, given a cosmopolitan character to production and consumption in every country.... All old-established national industries have been destroyed or are daily being destroyed. They are dislodged by new industries, whose introduction becomes a life and death question for all civilized nations, by industries that no longer work up indigenous raw material, but raw material drawn from the remotest zones; industries whose products are consumed, not only at home, but in every quarter of the globe. In place of the old wants, satisfied by the production of the country, we find new wants, requiring for their satisfaction the products of distant lands and climes. In place of the old local and national seclusion and self-sufficiency, we have intercourse in every direction, universal inter-dependence of nations. And as in material, so also in intellectual production. The intellectual creations of individual nations become common property."

The arrival of the global economic age calls for the emergence of "international ethics," thereby standardizing the economic behavior of humankind. Human society today has stepped into an age of all-around contacts, but mankind has not yet entered a time in which they do not worry about food and clothing, and the material resources are extremely abundant. There is a big gap between the developed and developing countries in terms of living standards. Human beings on the one hand have entered the age of all-around contacts, but on the other, they are engaged in contacts for each other's profits and livelihoods. Within a single country, inter-personal contacts not only need laws but also ethics; this is also true of international contacts, which need not only international laws but also international ethics. The establishment of international ethics meeting the needs of the 21st century will definitely conform to the exchange of the ethics of humanitarianism and "new utilitarianism." The basic contents of this international ethics should be one proceeding from the premise of mutual love, with human beings achieving their aim of each other's utility needs. Their most concise way of expressing this is: "extended love and shared benefit."

The international ethical principle of "extended love and shared benefit" is not in conflict with the uncompensated aid behavior of the "Red-Cross Society" of the international community, and not contradictory to the humanitarian aid of the United Nations. The latter is taken as the emergency disaster relief measure for guarantee of the international community and is a special incidence of the "extended love and shared benefit" international ethical principle. Their activities represent the lofty aspect of human beings' moral good, while the "extended love and shared benefit" principle is the daily ethical principle for international contacts and is a general principle. This ethical principle, in terms of its foundation, is established on the basis of "international law" and to remedy the defects in today's international community that lacks any daily exchange ethics. This ethics, at first glance, is not lofty and has daily practical characteristics. Under the actual conditions in which humankind has not eliminated and has difficulty in eliminating all class confrontations, the great disparity between the poor and rich, and regional differences, the use of a "formal rational" ethics to change the situation of having no ethical bottom line is more realistic.

4. Controlling Profits with Righteousness

The historical phase of the late Warring States Period and the early Han Dynasty was a time in which the concept of value in ancient Chinese society gradually took shape. The righteousness-profit concept formed in this historical period not only had a profound influence on people's lives during the various historical ages after the Han Dynasty, it also has influence even on modern Chinese society.

(1) Xun Zi's Righteousness-Profit Concept

Xun Zi was the one who epitomized Confucianism in the later part of the Warring States Period. To a certain extent, he was also a great thinker who integrated Confucianism and Taoism. His belief in "controlling profit with righteousness" exerted a great influence on Chinese society after the Qin and Han dynasties. In the eyes of Xun Zi, righteousness and profit are necessities for people. Even great sages, such as Yao and Shun, could not completely rid the people of their desire to pursue profits. Even the cruelest men, such as Jie and Zhou, could not entirely rid people of the desire to uphold justice. The only difference was that under the rule of Yao and Shun (early 21st century B.C.), the people's profit-loving hearts did not go against their moral hearts in abiding by the principle of righteousness, while in the ages during the reign of Jie (early 17th century B.C.) and Zhou (11th century B.C.), people's profit-loving hearts overwhelmed their justice-upholding hearts. Thus, as far as the ordinary people in society are concerned, it is alright for people to seek profits, but they must abide by some basic moral principles so that their profit-earning acts maintain moral righteousness.

Speaking from this angle, Xun Zi advocated a righteousness-profit concept that "gives consideration to both righteousness and profit." But Xun Zi also held that the tendency people presented at the level of their natural character was evil. He believed that all of the five sense organs have senses: The eye has the desire for color, ear has the desire for sound, nose has the desire for smell, and heart has the desire for not being refrained. If these are not put under check, they will conflict with each other and thus lead to social chaos. Therefore he demanded that society must use a moral principle to keep people's natural desire under check, thereby ensuring peaceful coexistence in human society. In this way, the relationship between righteousness and profit, as an ethical problem, is associated with the major political problems concerning the stability of the social-national order; thereby it becomes political ethics.

Xun Zi said, "The triumph of righteousness over profit means ruling the world, and the defeat of righteousness by profit means the disorder of the world." So he also advocated "controlling profit with righteousness." Precisely on this point, like Confucius and Mencius, he also opposed rulers competing for profits with the people, demanding that a ruler set an example in respect to morality. This ideological inclination can be said to be a common characteristic of pre-Qin Confucianism. Xun Zi said, "If the rulers at the top stress righteousness, then righteousness will triumph over profit; if the rulers at the top emphasize profit, then profit will defeat righteousness. Therefore, an emperor shouldn't talk about problems concerning the amount of wealth; dukes and princes should not say anything about advantages and disadvantages; senior officials and scholars should not talk about gains and losses; ordinary scholars should not engage in business; monarchs in possession of national land should not raise oxen and sheep; ministers dedicated to the emperor should not raise chickens, pigs, and other domestic poultry and cattle; those holding the official post of senior minister should not deal with interest on money; those holding the official post of grand master should not draw a circle to occupy any land or garden; those holding other official posts should take the seeking for profit as a shame and refrain from competing with ordinary people for profits in various trades and professions, and take it as a pleasure to distribute their wealth and feel ashamed if they accumulate a great deal of wealth."

Xun Zi opposed the outlook of officials in the various state departments who competed for profits with the common people, which is identical with the spirit of modern democratic political rules that demands that officials should not participate in market economy activities. The main functions of a government department are to keep the social rules. Its staff is much like the judges of various game activities, and a judge in any kind of game is not allowed to take part in the game. Therefore, the righteousness–profit concept of Confucianism represented by Xun Zi is not only a matter of personal cultivation involving a gentleman's personality, but also is a political ethical problem closely related to the rules of political activities.

On the matter of the cultivation of a gentleman's personality, Xun Zi followed Confuian ideology in maintaining that a gentleman should put righteousness first and be free from the temptations of profit. In the view of Xun Zi, the difference between a gentleman and a common man lies in this: A gentleman puts righteousness first, while a common man gives priority to profit. Only when one makes sure that "where there is righteousness, one does not tend to grab power and give thought to profit," can one become a real gentleman. The ideal personality of a gentleman initiated by Confucius and continued by Mencius, Xun Zi, and other pre-Qin Confucianists basically established the personality ideal of officials at the stratum of "Shi" (referring to officials and scholars) in traditional Chinese society, thereby forming an ideal ethical and political model that gives priority to moral righteousness. The personality ideal of these officials had a profound influence on and standardized every aspect of the internal affairs and diplomacy of the later empires. As a result, when traditional Chinese society encountered various other neighboring nations, it presented the image of a civilized nation that paid particular attention to social standards and therefore was acknowledged and emulated by other nations and countries.

(2) Dong Zhongshu's Righteousness-Profit Concept

Like Xun Zi, Dong Zhongshu (179-104 B.C.) affirmed the importance of righteousness and profit for people from an abstract sense, thereby advocating the giving of consideration to both righteousness and profit. He said, "Heaven gives birth to humankind, which automatically gives birth to two things — righteousness and profit, profit is used to rear people's bodies, while righteousness is used to cultivate people's hearts. A heart cannot feel happy without the nurse of righteousness, a body cannot have tranquility without the moistening effect of profit. Therefore, righteousness is specially used for nursing the heart, and profit is specially used for moistening the body."

On the question regarding which is more important, Dong Zhongshu followed the thinking of Mencius, holding that cultivating the heart is more important than rearing the body. He said, "No organ of the body is weightier than the heart, so therefore, nothing used to improve cultivation is more important than righteousness. Nursing a living body by righteousness outweighs rearing a living body by profit."

Compared to Mencius, Dong Zhongshu's understanding of the personalities of ordinary people was more practical. He maintained that although common people have good internal latent qualities, they are like seedlings rather than grown rice. The good quality in the personalities of ordinary people may show itself before it is developed by the wise rulers. Furthermore, limited by their intelligence, the common people often fail to see the long-term value of righteousness. When they are pursuing profits, they cannot hold back their pursuits, just like water that cannot be checked from its flow. Therefore, rulers set up dikes of propriety and education in order to prevent society from tending to get much profit and thus causing chaos.

During the Western Han Dynasty, when Dong Zhongshu lived, society began to experience the phenomenon of an increasingly serious polarization between the poor and the rich. Furthermore, Emperor Wu of the Han Dynasty intensified the social mood by chasing after profits for reasons of state interest, particularly for the purpose of stabilizing the frontier. Because of his deep-seated desire for long-lasting peace in the Western Han Dynasty, Dong Zhongshu put forward his thinking about the priority of morality. He said, "The benevolent one sets right his morality and does not seek personal profit. He cultivates rationality and is not eager for quick success." Later, the "Biography of Dong Zhongshu" in *The History of Han Dynasty* (《汉书》) changed these two sentences to read, "Putting it right and not seeking his own profit, comprehending the principle and not bothering about his merits." But the central meaning was not changed. Both require that a ruler take on the fundamental task of rectifying the rules of society and carefully safeguarding the social ethical principles while refraining from pursuing short-term material benefits. In terms of political theory, this topic is quite far-sighted, but it is extremely difficult to put it into a specific state policy.

Dong Zhongshu expounded the spiritual essence of the two concepts — benevolence and justice — from a theoretical angle, demanding that a ruler should adopt a benevolent attitude toward the people and a restrictive attitude toward himself. He said that the core idea in the *The Spring and Autumn Annals* (《春秋》) written by Confucius, lies in the question of how to handle relations between others and oneself. The fundamental law for governance of others and oneself contain two kinds of regulations: "benevolence" and "justice." Benevolence is used to manage others, justice is used to restrict oneself. The essence of the regulation of benevolence lies in affectionately loving others and not in deeply loving oneself; the regulation of justice lies in restricting oneself and not in containing others. If a ruler cannot restrict himself even when he restrains others, he cannot be regarded as living up to the regulation of justice. If the common people cannot widely enjoy a monarch's benevolence, the monarch cannot be called a benevolent monarch even when he deeply cherishes his own life. A person who only knows how to love himself, even if he holds the post of emperor or duke, will only be an ordinary man. Such a person needs not be eliminated by others, he will perish by himself. In this way, when Dong Zhongshu expounded on the matter of the relations between "justice and profit," he further explained the way for a monarch to proceed in personal cultivation. Thus he directly linked the matter of "justice and profit" with the policy of benevolence, thereby integrating the ruler's personal cultivation with the ruler's political ethics.

(3) *On Salt and Iron* (《盐铁论》) Reflects the Debate on Justice and Profit

In Emperor Wu's opening up of the frontier, he struck a blow at Hun's military force and defended the border areas of the Western Han Dynasty on the one hand, and on the other, he increased the state's financial burden. Therefore, in 81 B.C., this emperor of the Han Dynasty personally chaired an academic discussion on the state's economic policy. This was an individual case, a rare example of elite political democracy in ancient Chinese society. The emperor first demanded that the various prefectures and states recommend merchants and scholars to come to the capital city of Luoyang. Then he sent people to inquire of these people about the situation concerning the well-being of the people. These people resolutely opposed the government being the manager of the salt and iron industries. The government was represented by Sang Hongyang (152-80 B.C.), a statesman who resolutely favored government management of salt and iron. The merchants and scholars gave their reason as being the belief that the imperial court should not compete with the people for profits. Thus they opposed the government management of salt and iron.

Sang Hongyang, representing the state interests, stuck to his opinion that if the state did not control the salt and iron business, there would be no financial revenue to support the protection of the frontier, and at the same time it would be impossible to have sufficient wealth to attract people to serve as officials since the government lacked a cohesive force for society. In the eyes of later generations, both sides had their good points as well as their shortcomings. The problem was that the merchants and scholars were making use of the political ethics of Confucianist benevolence, justice, and morality as the weapon by which to criticize the viewpoint represented by Sang Hongyang, which put state utility above all else. But the people they were championing were not the common people and not even ordinary landlords; they were mainly the big merchants. The dispute between the exponents of government management and private management of the salt and iron industries reflected a contradiction between the government and the big merchants in the early period of the Western Han Dynasty. From this dispute it can be seen that the "debate on righteousness and profit" was not a matter of empty theory in ethics, but rather a practical issue closely related to actual political activities.

The theory put forward by the merchants and scholars was mostly influenced by the ideology of Mencius, but carrying with it their own special focus. Most of them did not understand the harm done to the border areas by the Hun. Despite its theoretical rationale, in the face of the grim facts surrounding the Hun's repeated invasions, it more or less presented the unrealistic view of scholars discussing politics. However, such arguement did not indicate that the government management monopoly was all rational. In fact, it was entirely possible to increase the state's financial revenue just by the method of increasing taxes on rich and big merchants. On the one hand, this might guarantee the result of enriching and benefiting people through the private management of salt and iron; on the other hand, it was possible to provide a full guarantee for state financial revenue, thereby reaching a win-win situation for the state and the people.

However, it is regrettable that the result of this dispute over the question of government management and private management of salt and iron was won by the state force represented by Sang Hongyang. The state used extreme administrative means to control the production of and right to sell salt and iron, thus eliminating free competition in the process of salt and iron production. In the end the result was a decline in the volume of salt production and in the quality of ironware, bringing an immense inconvenience to people's lives and taking away the interest of small merchants and peddlers and thus increasing the number of unemployed in society. Viewed from the results, the state did acquire immediate, short-term benefits, but the state also lost long-term benefits and the people gradually descended into destitution. From this typical incidence, it can be seen that the ethical ideology, in which the state should not compete with the people for profits, insisted by the Confucianists in "debate on righteousness and profit," finally, in fact, benefited the state. The ideology of enriching the people to make a powerful country possible is a rationalization contained in the Confucianists' "righteousness-profit concept."

5. Legitimacy of Profit-making Behavior in the Song, Yuan, Ming and Qing Dynasties

After Song and Yuan dynasties (960-1368), there were still two propositions in the "debate on righteousness and profit" within the Confucianist thinking. One advocated giving priority to the development of social utility; the other advocated putting moral suitability first. Because each of the two sides involved in the dispute failed to properly understand the intentions of the other side, the debate often turned into a dispute over personal loyalties. For example, during the Northern Song Dynasty (960-1127), Wang Anshi, a representative of the political reform school, put forward the idea of letting righteousness and profit run parallel and letting profit come first. He demanded an increase in the state's finance, thereby guaranteeing political stability on the northwest frontier. However, Cima Guang, who advocated "putting righteousness above profit," opposed weakening the economic strength of the local and powerful people through political reform. By the Southern Song period (1127-1179), some thinkers openly censured Wang Anshi, believing that he pursued profit to excess. This eventually led to the destruction of the Northern Song Dynasty. It was an exaggeration, of course, which did not conform to the actual historical facts. But from this it can be seen that attention given to maintaining the priority of social justice was the mainstream Confucian view during the Northern and Southern Song dynasties. Of course the country's military weakness during the two Song periods can neither be imputed to the exponents of utility nor to the exponents of justice. Rather it was associated with the military system and policy mistakes of the two Song periods.

(1) The Political Reform of Wang Anshi and His Righteousness-Profit Concept

Wang Anshi (1021-1086) was a famous political reformer in Chinese history. He was born into an ordinary, financially-deficient bureaucratic family of the Northern Song Dynasty. He had years of experience as a local official and a deep understanding of the life and well-being of the people. Furthermore, during the period when he served as a local official, he repeatedly worked for the interests of the public. Particularly during a period of famine, he used government power to require that the rich people make contributions for relieving the people in the stricken areas. In the eyes of those who advocated economic freedom, this practice was, of course, unreasonable, but in the traditional Chinese agricultural society, this conduct of working for the welfare of the public was welcomed by the broad masses of people at the lower level.

Wang Anshi's political reform was aimed directly at achieving more financial income for the country and at checking the profits of the big merchants, as well as striving for some economic benefits for ordinary peasants and landlords at the middle and lower levels. This kind of reform had some similarity to the question concerning government and private management of the salt and iron industries during the Western Han Dynasty. The role of Wang Anshi was similar to that of Sang Hongyang, while the role of Cima Guang was similar to that taken by the merchants and scholars. The concrete content of the Young Crops Law enforced by Wang Anshi was that the state-controlled granary issued agricultural loans to the peasants in early spring when the new crops had not yet come in and then retrieved the repayment at the time of the autumn harvest. The purpose was to control the exploitation of the ordinary peasants by the rich merchants, and to prevent the latter from exploiting the peasants through usury during the spring season when new crops had not yet come in. According to historical records, the decree pursued by Wang Anshi was aimed at helping ordinary peasants avoid famine during the early spring season. An official document of that time said, "Due to the situation of scarcity, people are often in the state in which new crops have not yet ripened and old grain has been used up. The rich people who practice financial accumulation take advantage of people's urgent need and ask for more than a doubling of the interest, while the people in urgent need are often troubled by their inability to buy the things they need. The goods stored in the country's granary are sold out only at times of crop failure and soaring prices, so that those who benefit from this are mostly urban vagrants. If the state can check and adjust the goods in each administrative region, selling them out at the time of high prices and buying at the time of low prices, thereby widening the channel for accumulating wealth and balancing prices, then the peasants can act in farming season with ease of mind, while the wealthy people with plans for financial accumulation will find it impossible to exploit omissions in the peasants' seasonal needs. What is done above is for the public; the country gains no interest therefrom."

The Jun Shu Law and Shi Yi Law (the law about buying and selling of goods and thus balancing prices, and the market trading law) pursued by Wang Anshi were also aimed at restraining the rich merchants from monopolizing the market, and preventing them from creating a situation in resistance to state power. In some of his articles on political reform, Wang Anshi repeatedly said that the implementation of the Jun Shu Law and Shi Yi Law is the right to put away and take in things and turn them into public ownership... Wealth is the thing that enables the world's people to unite; rules and regulations are the things that straighten out the order of world wealth; and officials are the ones who abide by the world's rules and regulations. If the qualities of the official ranks are not good, even when there are good rules and regulations, such officials will not observe them; if the rules and regulations are imperfect, even if there is wealth, it will be impossible to manage the wealth. If the existing wealth cannot be properly managed, then the people with the lowest position in the rural and urban areas can all create wealth and power by facilitating their money-making in accordance with their own intentions, and occupy the interests of all things by themselves alone, thereby competing with the emperor for the ruling power over common people. At the same time, they will indulge themselves in seeking their own endless desires.

Clearly Wang Anshi's economic reform ideology served to consolidate the central power of the state, and it opposed the big merchants who were contending with the state for power over the ordinary people. However, Wang Anshi's cleverness lay in the fact that, on the one hand, he tried to restrain the big merchants from scrambling with the state for ruling power over the common people; and on the other hand, he saw the positive role that the merchants played in the society and economy. He therefore tried his utmost to govern the big merchants through rational rules and regulations, thereby giving consideration to both righteousness and profit. He once said that he was sick of the behavior of the merchants and had to put them under control because they had become a too powerful force, and that the too powerful force of the merchants would eventually cause more people of the entire society to turn away from the foundation of agriculture. He also worried that if commercial business declined, the circulation of the world goods would be impossible. Thus he pointed to the need to enact laws and regulations to balance this. Later, in his memorial to the throne, Wang Anshi said, "Managing goods and wealth in the market means making unobtainable goods available on the market, and removing harm in time. If things in the market are not salable and are not in conformity with the people's needs, officials should buy things for their future needs. Such lines of action are not an expression of government monopolizing the profits. Because of the need to unite the country's people, it is impossible to exist without wealth; to manage the country's wealth, it is impossible to have no code of morality. If the wealth is managed by appropriate moral means, then the labor, ease, and comfort transferred must be balanced, the circulation of daily use goods must not be impeded, the abundance and scarcity of goods must be kept under management, and the judgment of the order of importance and control and decontrol must be done in a concrete way."

From this we can see that the political and economic reform carried out by Wang Anshi was not what his opponents criticized, and that his reform was aimed specially at chasing after profits without regard to the rule of moral righteousness. In fact, he only hoped to intensify the state power of control over society, so as to weaken big merchants' monopoly force in social and economic life. As a well-known statesman, he paid great attention to the restrictive role of morality in social wealth. The state interests he strove for, at least in terms of his personal subjective wishes, served the broad masses of low-level peasants. So, Wang Anshi's righteousness-profit concept contains the Confucian social ideals of equalization between the rich and the poor.

(2) Debate Between Zhu Xi and Yong Jia Schools of Thought

On the righteousness-profit question, Zhu Xi (1130-1200) mainly opposed selfish desire and personal relations in regard to personal moral character. He advocated that one should engage in all social activities out of the consideration of public interests. Therefore the debate on righteousness and profit was actually a debate on reason and desire and on public and private interests. In Zhu Xi's opinion, the debate on righteousness and profit was not only a theoretical problem, but a major matter concerning the rise and fall of a country. He said, "If there is difference in one's heart in seeking profit and respecting righteousness, then, there is difference in the rise and fall of actual efficiency. Scholars should deeply observe the differences and differentiate them distinctively."

In the ideological system of Zhu Xi, the "righteousness" he referred to was suitability as displayed by nature. The "profit" he referred to was the need as shown by human feelings. Chen Chun, a student of Zhu Xi, explained what is called the "desire in human feelings" in saying, "Desire means the intention to gain things, such as wealth and goods, reputation and position, and the ranks of nobility and official salary. These are only crude matters in profit. As regards the rise or fall and more or less what one bothers about is an expression of profit; acts taken to gain convenience for oneself are also profits. Pursuing a reputation, spying on efficiency, seeking for what one secretly wants, acting in compliance with human feelings, and having the idea of envying outsiders — all these are expressions of profit."

The great thinker Zhu Xi rejuvenated the Bailu School in the late 12th century. The rules of the school formulated by him influenced the development of Confucian teachings during the following 700 years.

Chen Chun explained "profit" in a narrow sense and a broad sense; profit in a narrow sense refers to various benefits visible in daily life, profit in a broad sense refers to all requirements related to a person's personal wishes.

In the eyes of Zhu Xi, "having a profit-making heart" for a person is actually the beginning of selfish desire, and selfish desire is contrary to the just demands of nature. Zhu Xi said, "The desire for profit is born out of the comparison made between a thing and the self. This is an expression of the selfishness of human desire. If people follow the requirements of nature, they will refrain from pursuing their own profits. Nature, on the other hand, does everything for their benefit. Becoming a victim of human desire, then, makes it possible for harm to come to them when they have not yet gained any profits."

On the question regarding the relationship between righteousness and profit, the core ideology of Zhu Xi puts emphasis on the priority of righteousness and the requirement that profit must be subordinated to righteousness. Under this ideological principle, he affirmed the positive role of "profit." So, his righteousness-profit concept can be understood from the following three aspects.

First, on the question regarding which is more important, righteousness or profit, Zhu Xi took the orientation of value by "putting righteousness above profit." He said, "With correct righteousness, profit will naturally come of itself; to give prominence to morality, then, efficiency will also naturally come of itself. If one worries only about profit or harm, one will not necessarily gain interest, nor efficiency."

Second, Zhu Xi stressed "controlling profit with righteousness." He said, "Benevolence is the virtue of the heart and the natural rule of love. Righteousness is a restriction on the heart and the appropriateness of things." While answering a student's question "How can a person perfectly handle affairs?" Zhu Xi answered, "Righteousness is like a knife, a sharpened knife that can cut off and shape other things. Once a thing appears before righteousness, righteousness will cut off the part not in compliance with the requirements of righteousness. The heart naturally has such a shaping ability. This shaping ability is as sharp as a knife or an ax, when things come, the heart chops them as is done with a knife or an ax. Those in compliance with the requirements come to this side, those not in compliance with the requirements go to that side."

Third, Zhu Xi stressed that a gentleman should give consideration only to legitimacy (righteousness) without regard to the existence or non-existence of profit. On this point, Zhu Xi's ideology was quite close to the pure obligation theory. His disciples had frequent discussions with him on the meaning of Confucius' assertion "a gentleman takes as much trouble to discover what is right as lesser men take to discover what will pay" in *The Analects*. Zhu Xi gave a very detailed answer, and he paid special attention to the question regarding "What should be done and what should not be done." In his opinion, the difference between a gentleman and a lesser man lies in: "A gentleman knows only what should be done and what should not be done, while a lesser man only bothers about advantage and disadvantage. A gentleman gives no thought to advantage and disadvantage. He is only concerned about what should be done in light of the requirements of Nature." Zhu Xi cited the need in daily life to make clear what "should be done" and what "should not be done." For example, if a silver coin is accidentally dropped on the ground by somebody and a gentleman sees it when he passes by, the first thing that comes to the gentleman's mind is that the coin belongs to another and that he should not pick it up as his own "profit." But if a lesser man sees this silver coin, he will think immediately that this is his "profit!" With no regard for whether it conforms to the principle of righteousness, the lesser man will pick it up and take it as his own, feeling at ease and being justified. From this example it can also be seen that while discussing the question of righteousness and profit, Zhu Xi paid special attention to whether people upheld the moral principle of "righteousness" at any juncture when they were faced with profit. He did not simply oppose people wanting to gain profits.

On the question concerning the relations between righteousness and profit, although Zhu Xi strongly stressed the priority of righteousness, he did not theoretically set out righteousness as being completely opposed to profit. Instead, he only regarded the relationship between righteousness and profit as one of being "between the head and the tail," or as what we might term today as the relationship between the first and the second. When one of his students said, "Righteousness is the appropriateness of the requirement of a natural principle, everything is only treated as rightful behavior as stipulated in the principle in which one's own selfishness will not be taken into consideration. Profit is something needed by human sentiment, it means a thing is done as required by one's personal intention or chosen to be done at one's convenience without considering whether it is required by principle." Zhu Xi gave an answer to this, saying, "The difference between righteousness and profit need not be mentioned in such harsh terms. The relationship between righteousness and profit is just like the one between the head and the tail. Righteousness means appropriateness. A gentleman thinks this thing should be done this way and that thing should be done that way. The things are done only after their appropriateness is determined. In this way, how can there be the happening of unprofitable things? A gentleman only considers righteousness, and will no longer consider what profit will come in the next step."

The concept that "a gentleman is indifferent to profit" that Zhu Xi mentioned here does not mean that a gentleman opposes profit. He only meant that as long as the question of righteousness is properly resolved, profit will come accordingly. On the contrary, if the aim is confined only to the pursuit of profits, a profit will not be finally gained and it will be lost in the end.

Zhu Xi and Chen Liang (1143-1194), representatives of the "Yong Jia school of thought," once had an intense debate over the issue of "righteousness and profit." The basic viewpoint of Chen Liang was that in daily and political life, it is possible to hold fast to the standard of "letting righteousness and profit run parallel, making miscellaneous use of the imperial rules." He pointed out that insistently using righteousness to restrain profit and the kingly way (benevolent governance) to restrict imperial rule (rule by force) is impractical in the specific historical course. Righteousness means the observance of certain kinds of rules embodied in the process of people's pursuit of profits. There does not exist abstract righteousness that stands above concrete economic activity. The kingly way is also expressed in the imperial rule.

To deal specifically with these viewpoints of Chen Liang, Zhu Xi wrote several long letters in which he discussed questions about righteousness and profit with Chen and wrote about the kingly way and the imperial rule. In Zhu Xi's opinion, none of the many major Confucianists after Mencius and Xun Zi to the time of the Han and Tang dynasties had clearly explained the problem concerning relations between righteousness and profit, and between the kingly way and the imperial rule. Only after the appearance of great thinkers such as Cheng Hao and Cheng Yi of the Northern Song Dynasty did the problem concerning these issues become theoretically clear. As Zhu Xi saw it, only by adhering to the ideological principle of putting righteousness before profit and using righteousness to control profit, was it possible for social and economic activities to generate a good social effect, otherwise social problems would emerge and social contradictions would arise.

The debate between Zhu Xi and Chen Liang came to no resolution in the end. Chen Liang stubbornly clung to his own beliefs and Zhu Xi could do nothing about this. Disputes between ideology and theory cannot be treated as a matter of who defeats whom by the use of any ordinary win-lose concept. They often reflect an attitude that human beings may take toward certain problems at a certain particular historical stage. Through theoretical debates, it is possible to reflect on the rationality and legality of our human behavior and to help human beings correct some deviations in practice.

(3) "The Principle of Honoring Others Is Righteousness; Use by Human Beings Is Profit"

Under the historical conditions of the 17th century, Wang Fuzhi, (1619-1692), one of the outstanding thinkers in traditional Chinese society, made a systematic and profound exposition of the "righteousness-profit" question. He opposed the thinkers and administrators who neglected people's interests and engaged in empty talk about moral righteousness, as well as the people who were only concerned about their own interests, immediate interests, and just a few people's interests, while neglecting the interests of people as a whole and long-time interests. Through his commentaries on *The Changes of Zhou*, the oldest Confucian classic, he pointed to "righteousness" as something heaven has bestowed on all things that seek their own convenience in line with their own special attributes. He said, "The Heaven lets all things, at the beginning of their emergence, each use what they have respectively been given as their due, either letting them keep quiet or letting them be active, or letting them live or die. Let them gain their benefits in light of the special attributes of concrete things so that each can be content with its original disposition and realize its own profit. It is not as if they took the initiative to pursue unimpeded profits after everything had been started. However, they worry that this is not in conformity with regulations and that they obtain profits only after making another choice."

For this reason, Wang Fuzhi greatly affirmed the importance of "profit" to people's material lives. He said, "The matter of having a meal is the foundation on which a sense of propriety is based. Profit is the foundation by which to reach stability for the people." So-called "righteousness" is a social norm that is helpful to people's rightful behavior. Such social norm has its natural rationality. He expressed this view: "Righteousness is the general term of the natural rule by which heaven and earth benefit all things, and the means by which people gain their due." However, in the eyes of Wang Fuzhi, "Righteousness is the norm that is helpful to people's behavior through taking advantage of the natural rule. If people can get their due from what they have done, then the natural rule is practical when it is popularized worldwide. So how can there be the phenomenon of disadvantage?"

Precisely because righteousness is so important, Wang Fuzhi strongly affirmed the importance of making a differentiation between righteousness and profit, and he affirmed the significance and positive role of justifiable "righteousness" in regulating people's profit-making behavior. He also combined the righteousness-profit issue with the political matter of "people's life and death and the country's misfortune and happiness." He said, "*The Changes of Zhou* notes that 'What is beneficial to all creatures is sufficient to coordinate various kinds of norms and make them harmonious.' Righteousness is sufficient to provide real value for human society; profit is sufficient to bring about coordination and harmony. The so-called coordination and harmony refer to unity, that is to say, there cannot be a profit without the regulation of righteousness. Nothing can be more advanced than such a view. This means striving to put righteousness into practice and staying away from the temptation of profit. Nothing more than the norm of righteousness is needed to play a role in controlling harm; nothing is more dangerous than pure profit that inflicts harm on people. Where pure profit can be controlled by the regulation of righteousness, harm will naturally be eliminated. There is no special truth involved here. It is only a matter of keeping pure profit at a distance. The difference between a wise man and a fool is the same as the difference between upholding righteousness and seeking profit; while the difference between upholding righteousness and seeking profit is the difference between gaining profit and suffering harm. Upholding righteousness and seeking profit will lead to people's life and death and the country's misfortune and happiness. There is nothing wrong with this."

In his excellent thinking as contained in this long passage of exposition on the relation between righteousness and profit, the "righteousness" referred to by Wang Fuzhi cannot be simply equated with the social moral standard, which is said to be opposed to profit by traditional Confucianism. Rather it is the necessary social norm that can promote social benefits and sustain development. Failing to understand the substantive content of the righteousness as mentioned by Wang Fuzhi is liable to confuse his thoughts with traditional Confucianism, especially with Zhu Xi's concept of putting righteousness above profit.

As a summarizer of traditional Chinese philosophy, the profundity of Wang Fuzhi's incisive views lay in his ability to discuss the complicated relations between righteousness and profit under specific social circumstances. In an age of the decline and chaos of politics and religion, upholding the principle of righteousness may not necessarily help one gain profit. Sometimes it benefits one thing, but it will not necessarily bring benefits to many other things; sometimes it benefits one individual, but it will not necessarily bring benefit to all the people of the country. Real righteousness must be "giving extended applications, applicable to others and oneself, to major things and minor things, to norm and adaptation. Furthermore, in considering their appropriateness, no concrete matter is improper, and none of the concrete cases is impeded."

When discussing the righteousness-profit issue, Wang Fuzhi broke out of the sphere of economic ethics and moral philosophy. He discussed the ethical relations between different ethnic groups from the angle of more general ethnic ties. He divided righteousness into three levels: A person's justness; one-time cardinal principles of righteousness; and the past and present general righteousness. The person's justness mainly referred to a minister's unconditional political loyalty to a monarch as shown in the politicized Confucian tradition. The one-time cardinal principles of righteousness mainly referred to a minister's political loyalty towards an enlightened monarch under a comparatively ideal circumstance, that is, the monarch the minister attends upon is "being served by the world's people to fit him as the master." The past and present general righteousness mainly meant that the overall interests of the Chinese nation required concrete content in Wang Fuzhi's ideology, that is that the principle of civilization represented by the Chinese nation holds the highest position and should not be impaired or ruined by neighboring ethnic minorities. These three levels of righteousness (ethical standards) sometimes can be highly unified. Under such a circumstance, it is possible to use the idea of "one-man righteousness" to judge whether a person's behavior is correct or not. When these three levels of righteousness cannot be unified it is impossible to use the "one-man righteousness" to judge the legality of a person's political behavior. The logical order is that "one-time righteousness" cannot be used to replace "past and present general righteousness" and "one-man righteousness" cannot be used to replace "one-time righteousness."

Although the "past and present general righteousness" elaborated by Wang Fuzhi, as seen today, has the tendency of stressing the superiority of the civilization of the Chinese nation, it contains a certain rational factor, that is, the overall interests of each nation, including the principle of civilization, is more important than the interests embodied in the imperial court during a given historical period. In the age of Wang Fuzhi, there was still no sense of the sovereignty of "a nation or country" as there is in the system of modern international law. Therefore, he could not clearly put forth the concept of the sovereignty of a nation or country as can modern people. But the "past and present general righteousness" that he talked about can be understood in this regard. At the present time when multi-level exchanges are being carried out between nations and countries, statesmen at the highest deci-sion-making level as well as those who take the welfare of all mankind as the object of their own theoretical solicitude, should precisely consider the political rationality and legality from the angle of the "past and present gen-eral righteousness" of the human society so as to put the immediate interests of human behavior and humanity's long-term future interests into a rela-tively coordinated relationship. This should be regarded as a contribution made by Wang Fuzhi, one of the most outstanding thinkers of China during the 17th century.

Yan Yuan (1635-1704), another important thinker of the Qing Dynasty, also made a systematic study of the question of righteousness and profit on the basis of carrying forward the spirit of pre-Qin thinkers, and in this he also made some advances.

First, he maintained that righteousness and profit are unified, and said, "Taking righteousness as an example was a natural and straightforward prin-ciple of the ancient sages. The matter of 'profit and use,' mentioned by Yao and Shun, was, together with 'virtue' and a 'better life,' regarded as three primary matters in *The Collection of Ancient Texts*. Profit and use contribute to one's steadfastness, can stabilize one's body and can regulate one's be-havior. All of these are roles played by profit. Therefore, profit is the coor-dination and harmony as shown between the norms of righteousness. The idea of 'profit' is mentioned more often in the book *The Changes of Zhou* than in *The Collection of Ancient Texts*. Mencius strongly denounced 'profit' mainly because he was averse to the unkind treatment of and heavy levies placed on the common people. Yet gentlemen greatly treasure the kind of profit that conforms to the norm of righteousness. Later, certain Confucian intellectuals took a contrary position in talking about 'putting right the norm of righteousness, and refraining from seeking profit.' This is overstated! Some people during the Song Dynasty liked to make such remarks in order to achieve their aim of covering up their empty and useless learning. I once tried to correct their bias and change their attitude as given above into this: 'putting right the norm of righteousness is to seek profit, giving prominence to the main principle is to consider its efficiency'."

Second, he criticized some Confucian scholars who lived after the Northern Song Dynasty and who separated the interdependent relations between righteousness and profit and who promoted righteousness and belittled profit, thus bringing harm to political life. He took the national subjugation of the Northern Song Dynasty as an example of this, pointing to the harm caused to state security as a result of the neglect of rightful profit. He said, "When they saw the action of inspecting and managing the frontier, the Song-dynasty people denounced it as being nosy; when they saw the action of improving the economic order, they censured it as amassing wealth; and when they saw someone carefully considering talent and force, they assumed a detestable attitude of denouncing such a person as a base man. If this practice was not changed, the entire world would have had no days of tranquility."

Living during the early years of the Qing Dynasty, Yan Yuan opposed the thinkers of the Confucian school of idealist philosophy in the Song and Ming dynasties who wallowed in an ideological atmosphere of pure moral norms. He also exposed, from a moral aspect, the hypocritical features of the thinkers of the Confucian school of philosophy of the Song Dynasty (the Neo Confucianists) who superficially talked about "seeking morality and not food." He pointed out that in fact "they nominally did so, while actually being content with any article they prepared for coping with an imperial examination, so as to suit this to the demand for fame and gain." Discussion of the relations between righteousness and profit at such a level had gone beyond the requirement of economic ethics, and had become associated with the question concerning the sincerity of morality and the philosophy of pure morality.

(4) Debate on Righteousness and Profit in Modern China

After 1840, Western economic capital, together with powerful military forces, intruded into China in all sorts of manner. Ancient China underwent a rapid change. In the face of the exceedingly grim reality, traditional disputes over "righteousness and profit" took on a new ideological content under the new epochal conditions. Yan Fu (1852-1921), a renowned translator in China who was the first to systematically accept modern Western ideas, put forward his own views on the question of "righteousness and profit." When he translated the book *Evolution and Ethics*, Yan Fu, based on

The Chinese version of the *Evolution and Ethics*, translation of Yan Fu, introduced Western thoughts to Chinese.

his understanding of the ideology of liberalism, made new explanations of the traditional Chinese "righteousness and profit concept." In his opinion, although there was some truth to the viewpoint of Thomas Henry Huxley (1825-1895) about the way a group protected itself for survival, this view was too narrow. In light of the common cultural experience of the East and the West, Yan Fu wanted to find a general rule for the study of "peace" for humanity. This "general rule of peace," he believed, should be the "obtaining of freedom for the people, with freedom for others as the boundary." Just as Adam Smith said: Where there is a big profit, there must be benefits for others. It is neither right to profit oneself at the expense of others, nor vise versa; it is neither right to benefit a superior person at the expense of an inferior person, nor vice versa.

From the above remarks we can see that Yan Fu accepted modern Western "rational egoist" thinking. Therefore, on the question of the "debate over righteousness and profit," he encouraged a "two profit" concept — public profit and private profit. In his opinion, "modern Western economics is an excellent example of righteousness and the ancient extreme man-nature rule, thus making it clear that the two kinds of profit are genuine profit." Proceeding precisely from the viewpoint of "simultaneously having two profits," he denied the thesis of a contradiction between righteousness and profit in both Chinese and foreign histories of the past and present. He said, "The word 'private-management' has been avoided as a taboo since ancient times and it has been all right to do so." However, private management varied with changes in the world situation. Generally speaking, the ancient people of both the East and West regarded utility as being contrary to morality. Good and evil things cannot be stored in the same vessel. Modern people say that according to the 'Sheng Xue' theory, one can live without private management. However, with the development of people's intelligence, we have come to realize that it is impossible to count one's merit unless one understands the rule, and it is impossible to seek profit without positive righteousness. When there is trouble with utility, just probe into the reason for the trouble and you will get the solution. So Westerners call this enlightened private-management. Enlightened private-management definitely does not run counter to morality and justice. What I call the science of handling the business of finance and accounting is the most useful learning for profit. This is because it is clear that two profits are profits, and one single profit definitely is not."

The "Sheng Xue" mentioned in this passage of Yan Fu's remarks generally referred to various kinds of economics relating to the production of material benefits. The "handling the business of finance and accounting" referred to economics in a narrow sense, and the "enlightened private-management" referred to the rational private production method encouraged by the capitalist economic system throughout modern history. This production method both affirmed the personal rational pursuit of economic benefit and required the giving of consideration to the improvement of social welfare. Of course, Yan Fu did not see the internal contradictions in the modern capitalist economy. He only described, from an ideal position, the rational aspect of modern capitalist economic ethics. However, this did provide a new train of thought for discussion of the problem of the relations between righteousness and profit in traditional Chinese philosophy from the angle of gaining both public profit and private profit. Because the traditional debate on righteousness and profit was only concerned with the relations between utility and morality, the thought that holds a leading position in the tradition of Confucianism affirms the priority of morality, requiring that people engage in all economic activities under correct moral norms. Yan Fu mainly discussed the relations between personal interests and social interests. Influenced by the moral concepts of modern Western utilitarianism, he held that the practice belonging to social interests conforms to the moral requirement of righteousness. This view was quite different from traditional Confucianism that upholds justice and belittles profit.

Influenced by modern Western views, Liang Qichao (1876-1929) also advocated the integration of "benefiting oneself" with "benefiting others." He gave new explanations to the old question regarding the traditional Chinese debate on righteousness and profit. First, he extended the traditional idea of "profiting oneself" into the idea of "profiting the group," and then he proceeded to combine the idea of "profiting oneself" with the idea of rights as initiated in modern Western society. He said, "None of the world's moral laws is not established on the basis of profiting oneself. In regard to birds and beasts, the righteousness concerning the importance of knowing different categories of creatures is only a matter of profiting oneself. The reason why humankind can dominate the world lies in its reliance on this. Advocacy of the righteousness of loving one's country and protecting one's race is aimed at profiting oneself too. The reason why the nationals can achieve progress and prosperity also lies in their reliance on this. So, if a person lacks the idea of profiting oneself, he will definitely give up his right and rush to throw away his responsibility, and he will finally fail to support himself."

In the view of Liang Qichao, the act of genuinely profiting oneself is one of respecting one's own right and is not selfishness at all. It does not necessarily conflict with the moral behavior of profiting others. He said, "The intention of profiting oneself and the intention of profiting others is a matter of integrated intention, not two separate intentions. Modern philosophers say that the human beings have two kinds of love: One is the original love of oneself; the second is a disguised love of oneself. The disguised love of oneself is actually a love for others. One cannot survive independent of others, so he must live among a group. In so doing, he, together with others, can jointly create a living environment; yet he must not enjoy profit alone in disregard of whether or not there is harm to the others. If there is, then harm will also come to the individual before he benefits himself. Therefore, the one who is good at profiting himself must first gain profits for the group, and then profit will come accordingly to himself."

Finally, Liang Qichao came to the conclusion that: "One who really can love himself has to extend the same love to his family and country, and has to extend the same love to his family members and his fellow-countrymen, so this gives rise to the righteousness of loving others. One's act of loving others also serves oneself. If one is well aware that the two, different in name, are from the same source, there will be no need to talk glibly about extended love intended for high reputation, or to avoid mentioning profiting oneself so as to deceive oneself. The practice of profiting oneself naturally becomes an act of loving others; increasing the capacity for loving others naturally can achieve the efficiency of profiting oneself."

Proceeding from his good wishes, Liang Qichao, trying to prove the unity of profiting oneself and profiting others, neglected the aspect of the inherent contradiction and conflict between personal profit and society. Like Yan Fu, he mainly wanted to prove the unity between personal profit and social interests, so as to provide proof of moral legality for the appearance of personal profits in modern Chinese society. Thus his views also contained the tendency of utilitarianism in the righteousness-profit debate.

(5) Southeast Asian Financial Crisis and the Justice-upholding Spirit Exhibited by the Chinese Government in International Economic Behavior

In January 1997, an American stock speculator launched an attack on the Southeast Asian financial market that he had long been coveting. The Thai financial market was the first to bear the brunt of this attack. In May of the same year, international monetary speculators began to undersell the Thai Baht. This currency collapsed in early July, and then the financial storm began to sweep Southeast Asia. October 20 was the 10th anniversary of "Black Monday," the American Wall Street Stock Market tragedy. On this very day, the Hong Kong stock market began to drop and on October 21 and 22, the Hong Kong Heng Sheng index fell by a big margin for two consecutive days, with the accumulated falling range approaching 1,200 points, which was described as a small stock disaster. On October 23, the Hong Kong Heng Sheng index dropped to its lowest point of 9,766.7 points, with the falling range reaching 1,871 points. The market value of Hong Kong's listing companies lost HK $433.5 billion on that day alone, HK $1,542 billion less than the peak market value of HK $4,335.4 billion in August of the same year. The sustained sharp drop in the Heng Sheng index was a drastic fall, and the huge loss shocked the world. At the same time the stock markets worldwide generally had a slump in the form of a vicious circle. On October 27, New York's Dow Jones index slumped to 554.26 points, the day witnessing the most tragic slump in history, thus leading to a mid-way automatic stoppage of quotations for one hour. The Tokyo stock market had a slump of over 800 points after the opening of quotation. On October 28, Hong Kong's Heng Sheng index was down by more than 1,400 points, with the falling rate reaching 13.7 percent.

Under such circumstances, the Western media predicted that the Chinese government would allow the devaluation of the Renminbi (RMB) in order to reduce export pressures. For example, the British weekly, *The Economist*, published an article holding that, affected by the Southeast Asian financial crisis, China would devalue the RMB. The article-claimed depreciation of the currencies of various Southeast Asian countries had increased the opponents' competitiveness and that China's export would be adversely affected if the trading revenue and expenditures situation worsened, and that the Chinese government might then consider devaluing its currency. *The New York Times* in the United States also said that China seemed to be a country most possibly affected by the Southeast Asian financial crisis.

However, the Chinese government did not stimulate exports by the method of depreciating the RMB as claimed by some Western media. Rather, the Chinese government maintained the trend of economic development through tapping internal potentials, speeding up the pace of economic reform, expanding domestic demands, and a variety of other measures. In order to maintain the Asian economic situation, the government of the Hong Kong Special Administrative Region, with the support of the Central Government, adopted a series of measures to stabilize Hong Kong's economic situation, which included increasing public investment and stimulating domestic demands. In the end, the Chinese government had not developed the domestic economy by using the most convenient method of depreciating the RMB. Proceeding from the general situation of Asian economic stability, the Chinese government upheld the moral principle of regional economic development, and did not allow the depreciation of RMB purely from a profit-making angle, thus making a tremendous contribution in fighting the financial crisis. In 2000, the growth rate of Hong Kong's economy reached as high as 10.5 percent, the highest growth rate for Hong Kong in 13 years. It was also the highest growth rate in Asia and the world at large. From this typical incident of modern economic development, it can be seen that China, as a country with a long history of civilization, while handling the problem concerning national interests and the moral principle for international relations, pays great attention to moral principle, and will not violate the moral requirements of international relations just for temporary national interests. This is the image of a big responsible country and the image of traditional China abiding by moral principles in handling its relations with neighboring nations.

Chapter IV

The Ideology of Traditional Chinese Medicine (TCM) and the Ecological Ethics of China's Peaceful Development

In a famous myth of ancient China, *Great Yu Harnessing Flood*, Gun, the father of Yu, failed to control a flood by blocking it. After the dikes and dams that he constructed had been destroyed by the flood, disaster followed. The failure of his father was a lesson for Yu and so he began to control floods by dredging the rivers in order to channel the water eastwards toward the sea, according to the topographical conditions. Because of this success in flood control, Yu was chosen to be the Emperor. After that the ancient Chinese people developed their philosophical attitude toward various natural disasters. This was a distinctive traditional ideology of ecological ethics that advocated conforming to Nature. It might be summarized as a "theory of organic ecology" featuring "union of heaven (universe) and mankind."

In the "theory of organic ecology" featuring "union of heaven and mankind," harmony is particularly emphasized in the treatment of the relationship between them. Ancient Chinese people regarded themselves as a member of all the creatures in the universe, therefore they always followed natural laws to moderately procure necessities for their lives. For example, their hunting, fishing, and felling trees were arranged according the seasonal conditions. After their nomadic way of life was replaced by agriculture, the Chinese paid more attention to following the natural rhythms in agricultural

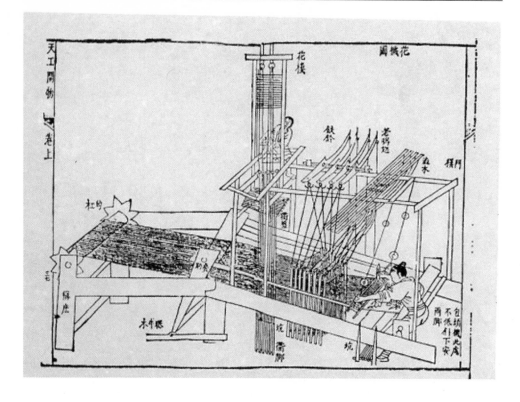

Creation of All Things by Heaven recorded technologies of ancient China before the middle Ming Dynasty.

production. They alternated the cultivation of crops according to the fertility of soil, producing "green fertilizer" by growing lucerne, and producing compost with the stems of grains following the harvest in order to improve the fertility of the soil. During the late Ming Dynasty, agricultural production in China had already reached its mature stage and material prosperity became better than it was in Europe at that time. Even though the Chinese people still lived simple and frugal lives, this was a good tradition established through a long-lasting agricultural development. Song Yingxing was a good representative of this outlook on life. As a great scientist during the Ming Dynasty, he said in his book *Creation of All Things by Heaven* (《天工开物》): "A velvet coat is made of the down from the bellies of hawks and the flanks of wild geese after numerous ones have been killed. How then can the owner put such a coat on?" This was a harsh criticism directed at those

148

people who unduly pursued gorgeous clothing. Although velvet was only a metaphorical term, it showed the passion of Song Yingxing for the lives of the birds and beasts in the natural world, much as the love for animals is shown by the animal protectionists in modern society.

Indeed, the relationship between Nature and humankind indirectly reveals the relationship among people. The natural sciences have developed from the separation of subjectivity and objectivity and this may help people to stand in awe before Nature. At the same time, it also brings about a tension between them. The tension between Nature and humankind is actually shown indirectly in the tense relationship among people themselves, which is brought about by the mode of production of modern capitalism in the Western countries. In establishing a modernized society in China, a large country with a vast population, we should not copy the developing pattern in the Western world. On the contrary, we should adopt the traditional Chinese view of organic ecological ethics, especially the philosophical belief in the "union of heaven and mankind" to instruct us in the construction of our modernized society with Chinese characteristics. Therefore, the exploitation and development of the theory of the "union of heaven and mankind" may provide tremendous value to Chinese people, a view that should be very useful to the peaceful development of Chinese society.

The theory of the "union of heaven and mankind" is composed of communication, interaction, and sharing of an ideology and morality between heaven and mankind. Among these the last concept is especially important to understanding the peaceful development of Chinese modernized society.

As a common sense in modern sciences and philosophy, "heaven" as a material entity has no consciousness. However, according to the viewpoint of the ancient Chinese people, the universe was full of spiritual features and the idea that a secret relationship existed between heaven and mankind was acceptable to them. The proposition of the "interaction of heaven and mankind" was first stated by Dong Zhongshu, a great thinker during the Han Dynasty. However, the theory of an "interaction of heaven and mankind" mentioned by Dong Zhongshu has by now lost its practical value. Yet some aspects in this theory, such as the "idea of a disaster punishment" may still provide us with some inspiration and warnings. In facing the overwhelming destruction of a natural disaster, we should make a self-criticism of the mistakes and even crimes made by mankind, rather than remain indifferent to them. According to Dong Zhongshu: "As an expression of the invincible might of heaven, natural disasters are really a punishment made by heaven on mankind. If humans are ignorant of such punishment, Nature would strike again.... In final analysis, natural disasters and various strange natural phenomena are always caused by the wrong political administration of the government." To make such an accusation probably seems unreasonable and dogmatic to contemporary people. Some natural disasters, for example, earthquakes and tsunamis, have no relation to the activities of human beings. However, the "idea of a disaster punishment" may help people reexamine their mistakes. To prevent disasters and provide prompt disaster relief is of course the responsibility of the government, and any delay or failure of the government to take efficient action should be certainly condemned.

The organic ecological view toward Nature developed from the long-standing agricultural culture of China certainly produced a positive influence on the development of the Western concept of organicism in philosophy. As noted by Dr. Joseph Needham, an English historian of science and technology, the Western organicism in philosophy can be traced back to Leibniz as its proponent in the Western world. Whether the establishment of his view began after he got the double obstacles out of the way, namely theological vitalism and mechanical materialism, or after he discovered the outlook of organicism held by the Chinese people is not clear. However, he was strongly inspired by the Chinese outlook (even if his view was not exactly derived from it) in making this ideological advance. According to Dr. Needham, the "monad" in the monadism of Leibniz corresponds to the "logic" of the idealist Confucians of the Song Dynasty. According to Needham, the monad system and its "predetermined harmony" similar to the innumerable and independent presence of "logic" in each model and organism. Therefore, the similarity between the theory of predetermined harmony and Chinese traditional ideology is much in evidence. Dr. Needham has raised this viewpoint for further investigation: "The Europeans acquired a benefit from Chinese organicism," which was first established by the philosophers of Taoism in 2nd century B.C. on the basis of their "concept of interaction," then developed into an integrated system by the thoughts of the idealist Confucians in the 12th century A.D., and finally served as an important tool to abolish the contradiction between theological vitalism and mechanical materialism in Europe during 17th century A.D. After the world outlook of mechanical materialism in Europe had been discarded by the people in modern times, "the modern natural sciences of Europe may acquire benefits from Zhuang Zhou, Zhou Dongyi, Zhu Xi, and other people of this sort."

The consumption of energy and water, especially petroleum, coal, and natural gas in the modern world may induce a worldwide crisis. The overwhelming development of the automobile industry and expansion of car consumption may finally bring human beings to a dead end. The acid rain produced by industrial waste has been a matter of great worry for people in some regions; and after too many trees have been cut down, the elevation of big river bottoms throughout the world through the deposition of sand has caused anxiety in many developing countries. During the 21st century, human beings must seriously pay attention to how best to exploit and utilize natural and regenerated resources with restriction. In this respect, the concept of natural organic ecological ethics developed from the long-standing agricultural culture in China may help people to reevaluate their opinions about production and consumption.

1. Traditional Chinese Medicine and Union of Heaven and Humankind

Among the empirical sciences, traditional Chinese medicine (TCM) is one of the most typical in showing and maintaining the characteristic ideology of the Chinese people. As an ancient science, the special thought about "wholeness" may show the relationship of human beings with Nature and with society. At the same time it may show the complicated dynamic relationship in the human body itself.

(1) The Zang Fu (internal organs) Theory of TCM and the Traditional Theory of Systematization

TCM is an ancient medical science with a long history and continuous development up to the present. The knowledge about construction of the human body, property of life, nature of disease and health, and therapeutic methods of TCM is still progressing and improving. In comparison with modern Western medicine, the viewpoints about human life in TCM are quite different from that of the Western world.

In general, the philosophic basis of TCM is the theory of the "union of heaven and mankind." It emphasizes both the internal relationship of the human body itself and its external relationship with the environment in order to understand and manage human life and its activities according to a concept of wholeness. Therefore, in the study of diseases and health, the complicated phenomena of the human body should be observed and analyzed with dialectical principles and logical methods. The healthy or diseased conditions of a human body may be determined by an examination of the ascent or descent of Qi, sufficiency or deficiency of Qi and blood, and the struggle between vital Qi (body resistance) and evil Qi (pathogenic factors). After the diagnosis of disease, a therapeutic plan can be developed and adequate drugs can be prescribed to a patient. The Zang Fu (internal organs) theory and ideology of human life in TCM are very important in the learning and practice of TCM. The treatment of diseases by physicians of TCM is often compared with the administration of political and social affairs by a government so that the philosophy related to political and social activities can also be used in the practice of medical services.

There are "five Zangs" in the human body, namely the heart, lung, liver, spleen, and kidney. The word "Zang" means invisible organs stored inside the body. These do not necessarily correspond to the internal organs with the same names as in Western

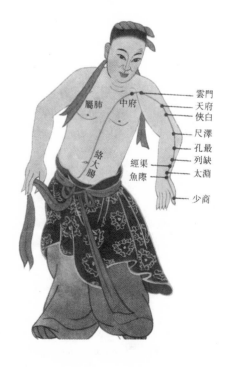

A painting of acupuncture points in TCM

152

medicine because they are not the "anatomical organs," but primarily a kind of "existing, functional 'five Zangs'."

In TCM, the "Fus" can be divided into two groups: the six "Extraordinary Fus" that take care of storage rather than transportation, and the five "Transporting Fus" that transport materials rather than store them.

The "Extraordinary Fus" are brain, marrow, bone, vessel, bladder, and uterus. All of them can store various materials without any leakage because they are produced from "essence of the ground," which is turbid and heavy in nature with a tendency to hold deposits, so they are in charge of the storage of rich resources.

The "Transporting Fus" are the five "anatomical-physiological organs, including the stomach, large intestine, small intestine, Sanjiao (three regions of abdominal cavity), and urinary bladder. All of them can receive, transport, and discharge various materials without delay because they are produced from "essence of heaven," which is clear and light in nature with a tendency to continuously move upward, so they are in charge of the constant discharge of materials just received. As explained by modern physiology, these are the internal organs that receive and digest food and transport and discharge the waste products of digestion. Besides the above-mentioned five "Fus," the gall bladder is added to make a complete system of six "Fus."

As mentioned in the "Plain Questions" of *On Five Zangs* (《素问·五脏别论》), "The six Fus can continuously transport food without delay, so that they are always filled with food, rather than being too full, ...after the food and drink are swallowed through the mouth, the stomach is filled up, but the intestines are still empty; after the food is transported into the intestines, the stomach becomes empty again. Therefore, this is why they are either filled up and not full, or full and not filled up."

As pointed out in the chapter "Miraculous Pivot" of *The Medical Classic of the Yellow Emperor* (《灵枢·黄帝内经》), "The six Fus can digest grain and water and distribute 'Jinye' (liquid nourishment)." In general, the six Fus correspond to the digestive and excretory systems of modern medicine. However, Sanjiao is a peculiar structure without any similar organ in Western medicine.

After the development and revisions made by medical scholars over successive dynasties in China, the Zang Fu theory of TCM can basically

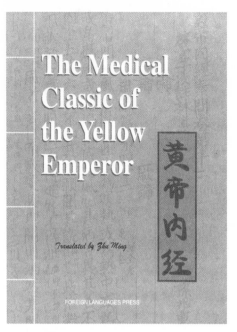

The Medical
Classic of
the Yellow
Emperor

Translated by Zhu Ming

FOREIGN LANGUAGES PRESS

The Medical Classic of the Yellow Emperor is China's earliest medical theoretic work.

explain the functions of various organs in the human body and the correlations between them. Among five Zangs, the "heart" is the most important organ, because it is the "origin of life." The heart can store spirit and control blood circulation through the vessels. Although medical scholars of the later dynasties developed some different explanations for the heart, none of them denied its leading position in the human body. As mentioned in the "Plain Questions," "The heart is the origin of life that causes changes of spirit." According to Zhang Jiebin (1563-1640), a great medical scholar of the Ming Dynasty: "The heart keeps the primitive spirit, as a source of sense to control all mental and psychological activities in human beings."

According to the principles of modern empirical science, contemporary physicians of TCM have produced some new explanations about the relationship between the heart and thoughts of human beings. Although the brain is recognized as the organ of thinking by modern medicine, the concept in TCM to attribute the control of thought to the heart is not completely nonsense because the heart is also the organ that controls the blood and vessels and acts as an energy source to keep the brain working. The so-called "sufficiency of heart Qi" in TCM may indicate a heart in a perfect condition both structurally and functionally, because it keeps the vessels full of blood to supply the brain as its energy resource. The traditional concept of the heart as an organ that controls thought and intelligence is also derived from its mobility (heart beat).

In TCM, the liver as a functional organ is considered as the "source of energy to relieve tiredness and keep people calm, keep the blood vessels unobstructed, and store the blood and soul." In modern medicine, the liver is

154

considered to be a solid organ to store blood and expel waste and toxic products. If the blood is deficient and the toxic products cannot be expelled in time, patients may not think in a clear manner. Therefore, knowledge about functions of the liver is almost coincident in both TCM and Western medicine.

In the other three Zangs, the functions are also clearly defined in TCM. As mentioned in "Plain Questions": "The lung is an organ to control the breath and preserve the 'Po' (corporal soul), a soul of Yang nature. The kidney is an organ to preserve the spirit with the function of hibernation and storage." In *The Medical Classic of the Yellow Emperor*, the spleen is considered to be like a granary and closely related to the stomach and the other five Fus.

The relationship between five Zangs and six Fus and between each organ of these two groups can be properly explained by the "Five-element Theory" of Chinese philosophy. As mentioned in "Plain Questions": "The heart is in an external-internal correlation with the blood vessels, under the control of the kidneys, and its brightness is shown in the face; the lungs are in an external-internal relationship with the skin, under the control of the heart, and their brightness shown on the body hairs; the liver is in an external-internal relationship with the tendons, under the control of the lungs, and with its brightness shown in the nails; the spleen is in an external-internal relationship with the flesh, under the control of the liver, and with its brightness shown on the lips; and the kidneys are in an external-internal relationship with the bones, under the control of the spleen, and with their brightness shown by hairs of the scalp."

Since the time of *The Medical Classic of the Yellow Emperor*, the Zang Fu theory has been supplemented by medical scholars during following dynasties. Chen Shiduo, a medical scholar of the Qing Dynasty, provided a new explanation about the relationship between liver, lungs, and heart: "The lungs belong to the 'gold' of the Five Elements and it cannot grow without 'wood' because in the theory of Five Elements 'gold' can conquer 'wood', so 'gold' cannot play its role if 'wood' is absent." Tang Rongchuan, another medical scholar of the Qing Dynasty said, "Liver belongs to the 'wood' of the Five Elements and tends to spread widely like the branches of a tree and keep things placid, orderly, and unobstructed. If this tendency of 'wood' is not suppressed, the heart and vessels are certainly all unobstructed. Another function of 'wood' is to promote passage and discharge after food and drink are taken into the stomach. The 'wood' element in liver can promote digestion, transformation, transportation, and discharge from stomach; if the clear Yang Qi (active function) is blocked from rising to help the stomach, the transportation and discharge of food may be suppressed and people may suffer from a distension of the stomach." Western physicians will treat patients of stomach distension with drugs to improve their digestive function without paying any attention to the influence of the liver. Therefore it is reasonably scientific for physicians of TCM to emphasize the complicated relationship between the five Zangs and the way they preserve the proper vitality and practical value, even though Western medicine at present occupies a dominant position in the medical field. For example, in the clinical practice of TCM, the treatment of nervousness, fury, and other emotional disturbances is achieved by relieving the stagnation of liver Qi. This usually produces a good therapeutic result. Because the theories of the Five Elements and Zang Fu have been discussed in detail in various TCM books, the author of this book has omitted further discussion about the relationship between the Five Zangs.

In brief, the wholeness and systematization of an organism has been superbly studied and discussed in TCM. This concept of organic wholeness of life was derived from the ideology of the "union of heaven and mankind" and the theories of Yin-Yang and the Five Elements of traditional Chinese philosophy. The knowledge about the relationship between human life and the Five Zangs, Six Fus, blood, Qi, and spirit are still not very accurate as evaluated by the criteria of Western medicine. However, Western medicine pays too much attention to the functional independency and isolation of the organs in the body and emphasizes the control of a single pathogen in the treatment of disease. In confronting each other in the new era, both medical schools should seriously examine the superiority and inferiority of itself. As for TCM, it may be better to get rid of the ancient imagery about the organic integrity of human life. At the same time, the modern philosophic ideology and scientific technology in fields such as biology, biochemistry, quantum physics, optics, information theory, and systematics may need to rebuild a new theoretical system about the organic integrity of human life. At the same time, Western medicine may make use of the classical logical thoughts about the organic integrity of human life to correct the defects originating from mechanical materialism and reductionism.

(2) Essence, Qi and Spirit: a Three-dimensional Ideology About the Creation of Life

The concept of the organic integrity of human life in TCM is not derived from modern scientific anatomy (although TCM also has some anatomical knowledge itself) but from ancient Chinese philosophy, especially that recorded in *The Book of Changes*, written before the Qin Dynasty and from the theories of Yin-Yang and the Five Elements. The theories were described in *The Medical Classic of the Yellow Emperor* in detail. Before the introduction of Western medicine into this country, the basic theories and ideology about the organic integrity of human life remained almost unchanged in substance with only some minor modifications made by later medical scholars.

As far as the origin of life is concerned, as for all things in the world, this was composed of Qi. As written in "Plain Questions": "It appears as Qi in the sky, then changes into Xing (form) on earth so that all things in the world are produced by a transformation between the Qi and Xing." Again, "The universe is wide and empty, and originated from the sky in which nine huge stars hang and seven shiny stars rotate constantly, but under which all things are produced from both genuine Qi, widely spread everywhere, and the Five Elements that change constantly. As a result, there are Yin and Yang; softness and hardness; darkness and brightness; and four seasons with weather that varies between hotness and coldness. After the appearance and continuous transformation of life, various species of organisms came to the world and made it prosperous." This was also discussed in detail in the "Plain Questions": "People are born on earth, but their lives originate from heaven. Human beings are created by a combination of Qi from both heaven and earth. Therefore these are the parents of people and help them adapt to the changes of seasons." As mentioned in the "Miraculous Pivot": "People will eventually die if they lack Qi."

It was further explained by Zhang Yuansu (1131-1234), a medical scholar during the Yuan Dynasty: "Qi is the master of Xing, mother of the spirit, origin of the three great *Cai* (heaven, earth, and human beings), source of all things in the world, and also the cause of change in doctrine ... so that an organism may be born after the transformation of Qi and altered after the change of Qi. It may be strong if Qi is excessive or weak if Qi is deficient, healthy if Qi is normal, or sick if Qi is abnormal, and dead if Qi is exhausted." In Zhang's statement, "spirit" is a general term for mental activities; the "three great *Cai*" means the three basic entities of heaven, earth, and human being; and the Qi is a very delicate and mobile material without definite form, a fundamental element to produce essence and spirit for human beings. Therefore, the concept of "Qi" is not only a theoretical element of ontology in Chinese philosophy, but also a philosophic basis for TCM and a metaphysical basis for the traditional Chinese sciences of life. The idea about creation of human life in TCM cannot simply be turned into reductionism because "Qi" is regarded not only as a delicate material but also as energy and movement.

In traditional Chinese philosophy, mankind is believed to be the "center" of the three great *Cai*, and in TCM the "spirit" is correspondingly the "center" of life among the three components, namely essence, Qi, and spirit. The anatomical organ that corresponds to the "spirit," or "center" of life, is the heart. The Chinese ontology of Qi accepts the concept of the materiality of the whole world, but refuses the idea of looking at objective materials as dead matter outside the human body that lack spiritual properties and are isolated from human beings. TCM accepts the philosophic concept of the ontology of Qi and looks at human life as an objective biological entity visible, intelligent and tangible. At the same time, it keeps to an intimate linkage with all things in the world by means of the delicate Qi. This is the superiority of the basic philosophic theories of TCM.

The basic elements that create human life in TCM are mainly essence, Qi, and spirit. As said in the "Miraculous Pivot": "Human life is made up of 'blood Qi', essence, and spirit that play their role in both the physiological and mental life of human beings. Ordinary Qi in the natural environment is transformed into 'blood Qi' after it is inspired into the human body." Different from genes that are regarded as the basic components of human life, TCM attributes blood to be the basic material that creates human life.

Therefore, an analysis of blood in the human body may be considered as the starting point for a profound study of the laws of human life in TCM.

What is "essence" in TCM? According to the explanation provided in the "Miraculous Pivot": "The essence is considered as the basis in creating human life."

The essence is the primitive material that creates human life. According to the "Miraculous Pivot": "Before the creation of human life, the essence is produced, then the brain is formed, then the bones as supporters, the vessels for the transportation of nutrition, the tendons for rigidity, flesh as the walls, and the tough skin with hairs for protection of body." What is essence in TCM for Western medicine? How can the human life be created by essence? It is impossible for TCM to give an answer. The only possible answer is a statement cited from the "Miraculous Pivot": "Human life is created by the interaction of the essence of life from both sexes, known as 'spirit,' because the process and result of the interaction of essence are an unfathomable mystery. The interaction and combination of the 'will' of both sexes may produce 'essence' first, and then form the visible human body after the creation of human life."

In brief, as an element for the creation of human life, "essence" is a delicate material of Yin nature, namely the primitive material of life in both sexes. Therefore, it is similar to the material with a chemical structure of double spirals of ribonucleic acids and the popular names of sperm and ovum in Western medicine.

Then what is the Qi used to create human life? As written in the "Miraculous Pivot": "The upper Jiao of the three Jiao (the upper Jiao refers to heart and lung; the middle Jiao spleen and stomach; and the lower Jiao liver, kidney, bladder, large and small intestine) can produce a dispersing effect to distribute the nutrients of grains from the stomach to the whole body, including the skin and hairs, as the delicate fog and dew of Nature irrigates various plants, so it is known as the Qi of life." The material carrier of Qi is the blood, but not the blood alone.

In fact, as a component of human life and in a more profound sense, Qi contains essence. Qi is also a delicate material that communicates between human life and all things in the universe. It can be divided into two groups. In a narrow sense, the Qi of life contains essence, saliva, liquid, blood, and vessels in the human body; and in a broad sense it contains wind, chill, summer heat, dampness, dryness, and the heat of natural weather. The Qi of the human body can be divided into four varieties: the first is the flowing delicate material, such as primitive Qi and nutrient Qi from grains and drinks; the second is the functional activity of the Zangs and Fus, such as the Qi of the five Zangs, six Fus, and meridians; the third is the pathological symptoms of the Zangs, Fus and meridians, such as failure of the lung Qi to descend and an upset of the stomach Qi; and the fourth is the abnormal materials that accumulate in the body, such as stagnated Qi, damp Qi, and fire-heat Qi.

In TCM, "spirit" can also be divided into two groups: in a broad or narrow sense. In a broad sense, spirit indicates human life and its external expression, as described in the "Miraculous Pivot": "The competition of essence from both sides (man and woman) is known as 'spirit'." In a narrow sense, it contains consciousness, thought, memory, imagination, emotion, sensation, sensitive responses to the changes of external environment, and the automatic control of the functional activities of all the organs in the human body. The medical scholars of later dynasties divided "spirit" once again into five varieties: namely spirit, soul, corporal soul, will, and ambition as the "five spirits," controlled by the five Zangs, and among these, will and ambition are spirits at a higher level, called the "superb spirit." As said in the "Miraculous Pivot": "Ambition and will can regulate spirit, keep the soul and corporal soul calm, adapt to coldness and hotness, and adjust emotions. If ambition and will can be maintained in proper order, the spirit may be active and cheerful; the soul and corporal soul may be stable; emotions may be under control, and the five Zangs can resist the attack of pathogens." Zhang Jingyue (1562-1639), a medical scholar of the Ming Dynasty, made a clearer explanation for the spirit: "Spirit can be divided into two varieties, one is Yang in nature called the 'soul' and the other is Yin in nature called the 'corporal soul.' In addition, will, worry, and all psychological activities are included in the 'spirit.' Generally speaking, the spirit is stored in the heart, and all mental and emotional activities in the human body are controlled and adjusted by the heart."

If the creation of human life in TCM is explained by modern scientific conceptions, essence, Qi, and spirit may be considered as self-regulation

160

processes of human life at three different levels, namely the vital material, vital power (function), and vital information. "Essence" is the primitive material of human life, because it is Yin in nature; "Qi" is a delicate material scattered and mutually transmitted between human body and Nature like fog or dew and participating in the transformation of materials in the human body; and "spirit" plays an important role in the self-adjustment of mental, emotional, and other psychological activities. Qi and spirit are Yang in nature, because they are active and closely related to the visible activities of the human body. As to the relation of these three elements, essence, Qi, and spirit may be considered as "one master and two servants" with the mutually opposing and integrating relationship of the Yin-Yang theory. If they are analyzed from the relationship between Nature and mankind, Qi is the master and essence and spirit are the servants. If they are analyzed from the self-sufficiency of human life, essence is the master and Qi and spirit are the servants; and if analyzed from the self-adjustment of human life, spirit is the master and Qi and essence are the servants. Therefore, the three-dimensional analysis of the complicated coordinating and coexisting relationship of these three elements may be used to explain their roles in creating human life. However, because of the complexity of diseases in clinical practice, the opinions about which one of these elements plays a chief role in the induction and development of diseases is quite varied. Therefore, the theories of TCM are very complicated!

When the three elements jointly create human life, what is the relationship between them and five Zangs, the functional organs of the human body? As said in the "Miraculous Pivot": "The five Zangs are organs to store the essence, spirit, 'blood Qi', soul, and corporal soul; and the six Fus are organs to digest and transport grains and drinks and to distribute nutrient fluids to all the organs in the human body."

The functional activities of five Zangs can also be affected by the spirit, the subjective mental status. If the spirit is normal and the will and ambition are not suppressed, the soul and corporal soul will not be disturbed or emotions upset, and then the five Zangs can resist any invasion of external pathogens. Therefore, the mental status can also affect the corporal functions of the human body.

In brief, the theoretical system of TCM concerning the creation of human life is composed of three elements, essence, Qi, and spirit. As compared with other corresponding theories of ancient medicine of other ethnic groups, it shows certain superiority in explaining the most complicated phenomena of human life. Even with the highly developed modern sciences and technology, Western medicine cannot completely replace it with modern theories. This is not only because the theoretical system of TCM is reasonable and practical in terms of clinical practice, but it is also due to the limitations of Western medicine in solving many difficult problems of life. Nevertheless, the theoretical system of TCM may serve as a useful supplement to the theories of Western medicine. Of course, in order to develop TCM, the unique traditional theories of TCM must be continuously preserved in order to be applied. At the same time, the achievements of modern sciences and technology should be also applied to improve the older ideas about the organic integrity of human life to a new scientific standard.

(3) Ideas About the Prevention and Treatment of Diseases in TCM may Serve as a Guide for Modern International Political Relationships

In TCM there are some very brilliant expositions about causes of diseases. Both the internal harmony of the human body and the adaptation to the external environment are emphasized in order to keep the health of the human body. The destruction of internal harmony and loss of balance between the human body and the external environment is the initial step in any change from health to sickness. Therefore, the importance of the harmony in the human body and its balance with the external environment is much emphasized in TCM as a practical science. In *The Medical Classic of the Yellow Emperor*, healthy people are called "balanced" people, balanced between Yin and Yang. As related in "Plain Questions": "During a complete breath, the pulse may beat five times, if followed by a sigh, and this is a normal manifestation in 'balanced people;' if an inhalation or exhalation is accompanied by just one pulse beat, this may appear in 'people with less Qi;' if an inhalation or exhalation is accompanied by three pulse beats, this may be present in 'people of febrile disease' with anxiety and a hot feeling one foot away from the arm; if an inhalation is accompanied by four pulse beats, this indicates death." In ancient times, as distinct from modern diagnostic measures, pulse diagnosis alone was used to examine the internal conditions of the human body. It can marvelously and successfully make a diagnosis and prognosis of a disease.

What are the pathological causes of diseases? As related in the "Miraculous Pivot": "All diseases are caused by wind, rain, chill, summer heat, emotional disturbances such as extreme joy or fury, diet and housing environment. Extreme fright and sudden fear may cause an isolation of Qi and blood, disturbance of Yin and Yang, obstruction of meridians, stagnation of the circulation in vessels, mutual contradiction between Yin and Yang, retardation of Wei Qi (part of Qi in nature of Yang, originated from spleen and stomach) flow, emptiness in meridians and vessels, and failure of Qi and blood distributing throughout the body. Then the human body breaks away from its normal condition."

In the "Miraculous Pivot," the causes of diseases were discussed in detail by the Yellow Emperor and Bo Qi. In order to answer a question of the Yellow Emperor about damage to the different organs by different external pathogens, Bo Qi analyzed the causes of Yin diseases and Yang diseases by dividing the human body into upper, middle, and lower parts. He said, "Without feebleness inside the human body, the external pathogens such as wind, rain, chill, and heat cannot affect the human body by themselves alone. The sudden attack of a strong storm does not produce disease in people when their bodies are not feeble. People may contract a disease only after the attack of invasive pathogens on a feeble body. If people are strong and robust, no pathogens can attack them. Severe diseases are mostly caused by both an attack of bad weather and feebleness in the body as a result of the combining of excessive external pathogens with a deficient internal resistance in the body." The Yin diseases are caused by emotional disturbances and an irregular life style, or as Bo Qi said, "The heart may be injured by worry, liver injured by fury, spleen injured by an attack of strong wind or sexual intercourse after drunkenness combined with sweating, and kidney injured by exhaustion or bathing after sexual intercourse combined with sweating."

In TCM, the balance of the human body is particularly emphasized because a change in the external environment is out of control of human beings. The ideas about the development of disease may significantly enlighten and encourage contemporary people in trying their best to improve their bodily immunity and keep away from the sources of disease.

As an achievement of traditional science, the concept about the causes of disease in TCM is quite reasonable and valuable. The origin of all diseases is always an attack of wind, rain, chill, summer heat, dryness, and dampness applied to our feeble bodies and caused by emotional disturbance. Therefore, a disease is produced by a combination of external violent pathogens combined with internal reduced body resistance. In pathogenesis, there are two sources of pathogens. They are either external or internal. As said in the "Plain Questions": "Pathogens may be derived from either Yin or Yang. The Yang pathogens are produced by wind, rain, chill and summer heat, and the Yin pathogens are derived from emotional disturbance, poor diet, and life style." Therefore, people must take care of their health and keep themselves away from pathogens by the adequate elimination of pathogens from both sources.

Besides the Yin and Yang pathogens mentioned above, sometimes psychological factors may also produce diseases. According to the "Miraculous Pivot": "Sometimes old pathogens may remain in a human body until stimulated and awakened by a mental disturbance. This may disturb the blood circulation and promote a combination of external and internal pathogens to produce mild symptoms not even detectable by eyes and ears. The pathogens are as mysterious as ghosts."

After an analysis of the external environment, internal Zang Fu, and psychological factors, TCM developed the basic theories about causes and development of diseases. At the same time TCM abolished the superstition that diseases are the punishment of gods and ghosts. According to the "Plain Questions": "We should not discuss the highest achievements of medicine with people who are bound by a belief to gods and ghosts." This shows that the theories about the causation of diseases are derived from the scientific epistemology used by TCM as its philosophic foundation.

From the theories related to the causation of diseases, TCM physicians further studied the superficial symptoms in the human body and arrived at the conclusion that diseases are mostly recognizable. Again as said in the "Miraculous Pivot": "The examination of external symptoms may show the condition of internal organs and further reveal the nature of a disease."

In the "Miraculous Pivot," the Yellow Emperor and Bo Qi discussed ways to understand the disease inside a body through observation of its external expression. In comparison with the political administration of the government, Bo Qi said: "The external expression of a disease can show the actual nature of the internal disease, just as all things on the earth, although in a shadow, may be as bright and clear as the sun and moon; the reflection of all things in a mirror or on the surface of stable water may show their appearance without any loss of exactness; the sound produced by beating a drum and its echo are exactly the same and coincident." From this statement of Bo Qi, the Yellow Emperor found a similarity between medicine and politics, and so he said with deep feeling, "In general, the five tones in the Chinese musical scale system, dou (宫), ri (商), mi (角), sou (征), and la (羽), are not apparent, nor the five colors, red, brown, greenish blue, blue, and purple. The five Zangs, heart, lung, liver, spleen, and kidney move and rock, interacted to each other just like those tones or colors. The close relationship between internal status and external appearance of a patient is just like that between a drum and drumstick, sound and echo, and a substance and its shadow. Therefore, the observation of external appearance from a distance may estimate the internal actual status; and nearby inspection may lead to a clear understanding of the mechanism of internal changes and predict their expression as shown on the body surface."

Through clinical practice over a long time, TCM physicians developed a system of diagnostic methods that included inspection, listening to and smelling, inquiring, and monitoring the pulse. As stated in *The Medical Classic of the Yellow Emperor*: "Inspection by the eyes can recognize a disease, detecting the minutest details, which are as clear as things in the light of the sun and moon. This is the highest approach. The palpation of pulse is regarded as a magic technique; and the inquiry of symptoms and daily life of patients can be easily done by all common craftsmen."

TCM physicians usually pay more attention to preventing than treating diseases, and they believe that "the best physician will cure a disease before its onset." As said in the "Plain Questions": "The wise physician always treats a disease before it assumes shape rather than after it has already taken shape, just as a country should be adequately administered before the occurrence of any riot." The treatment of a disease before it takes shape is much like digging a well before one feels thirsty or manufacturing weapons before a war starts. Otherwise it may already be too late! It is the fundamental principle of health care in modern medicine to prevent disease before its onset. Therefore, in *The Medical Classic of the Yellow Emperor* there are so many good ideas about health care that can also be valuable in the practice of modern health care.

The ideas of health care in TCM clearly reflect the positive attitude of the Chinese people in obeying natural laws for the establishment of a harmonious relationship with the natural environment. As said in the "Miraculous Pivot": "For health care, wise men would always try to adapt to the change of weather in the four seasons, keep their emotions under control, make their house safe and quiet, and adjust their mood in accordance with changes of Yin and Yang in rigidity or flexibility. If they do this, evil pathogens cannot attack their bodies and they may live a long life."

Both sickness and health are ordinary statuses of the human body. In social life it is impossible to find all people in a "balanced (healthy) status." Through clinical practice over a long time, TCM physicians have established two therapeutic principles: One, treatment of disease according to its pathogenesis; two, applying integral adjustment and treatment.

In the "treatment of disease according to its pathogenesis," the "pathogenesis" is the reason for diseases to occur, develop, and change and to rely on treatment. In "Plain Questions," Bo Qi said, "The key principle for the treatment of disease is to accurately judge the developing stage of disease in order to avoid missing the time of treatment when the activity of Qi and blood are still in their most active status." He added, "Try to carefully follow the developing stage of disease, keep it in a curable condition, find the external pathogens or diseases causing internal damage, adjust the overexciting or very depressive condition of the five Zangs, restore their original balanced status, and promote the circulation of Qi and blood. Then the body may finally return to a harmonious balance."

In clinical practice, the principle of "treating the same disease with different methods" is derived from the idea of the "treatment of disease according to its pathogenesis." This indicates that the same disease should be treated differently according to its severity and to geographical differences. According to the "Plain Questions": "In the same disease suffered by people at different locations, the excessive toxic heat in northerners should be expelled, and the accumulated cool Qi in southerners should be driven out. In the treatment of this disease, the warm-dispersal method is used for northerners, but the astringent method is used for southerners to drive out the cool Qi by raising warmth in their body. The same symptoms in a disease of different severities should also be treated differently." In "Plain Questions," the Yellow Emperor asked, "In the treatment of a cervical abscess, why do some surgeons cut it with a sharp stone edge and others perforate it with a needle? In both cases the person is cured." Bo Qi answered, "It is due to the difference in the severity of the abscess. During the developing stage, the abscess should be pierced with a needle to slowly discharge the toxic pathogen; but after the blood has accumulated with an excessive toxic pathogen, the abscess should be incised with a sharp stone edge so as to drain the accumulated pus. This is the reason to treat the same disease with different methods."

In "integral adjustment and treatment" there are two principles: first, the "integral adjustment and treatment" between heaven and mankind; second, between the mind and body. Following the first principle, physicians should examine the relationship between the patients and their surrounding environment and treat them according to time, place, and the condition of the patients themselves. In the "Plain Questions," the close relationship between the physiological activities in the human body and the natural environment were discussed in detail: "On shiny and warm days, blood is thin, moist, slippery, flows easily, and leaks out, and the Ying Qi (nutrients) and Wei Qi (body resistance) tend to float upward and the Qi in the body flows easily. On cloudy and cold days, blood is thick, sticky, and flows sluggishly and the Ying Qi and Wei Qi tend to descend downward. In accordance with the crescent moon, the blood and Qi begin to increase in quantity; as the moon gradually becomes fuller and fuller, the blood and Qi become richer and richer and the muscles become more and more elastic; as the moon gradually reduces in fullness, the muscles become less elastic, the meridians become empty, and the Ying Qi and Wei Qi tend to scatter away, although the appearance of the human body remains unchanged. Therefore, blood and Qi should be adjusted according to the changes of the seasons. For example, acupuncture treatment in a cold season is prohibited, but it may be applied without hesitation in a warm season; method for discharge should not be applied during the crescent moon period whereas nutrition is not necessary during the full moon period; and the application of treatment is unsuitable during the period without a moon. This is a concrete statement about the application of "integral adjustment and treatment." In fact "integral adjustment and treatment" may be used in the treatment of many diseases, and so TCM is also called a "balanced medicine."

In TCM, the principle of "integral adjustment and treatment for both physical and mental disorders" is closely related to the concept of organic integrity in human life. In *The Medical Classic of the Yellow Emperor*, the human body is considered to be an integral entity with Zang Fu as its center and Qi and blood in its meridians as messengers to integrate the corporal body with mental activities. Therefore, in clinical practice, physicians must carefully examine and study the interrelation and mutual influence between the corporal body and mental activities as well as among the Zang and Fu. In brief, the principle of "integral adjustment and treatment" can be summarized as follows:

(i) Treatment of local lesions by integral adjustment and treatment of the Zang and Fu: The local lesions can be cured by treatment applied to their corresponding Zang and Fu because there is a close relationship between them. For example, the liver and eyes are closely related so that blurred vision can be cured by treatment applied to the liver.

(ii) Treatment of disease in a Zang by the integral adjustment and treatment of another Zang. The disease of a Zang can be treated by mutual promotion or suppression applied between the Zang and Fu. In "Plain Questions," the "integral adjustment and treatment" between five Zangs was discussed in detail. For example, the liver may be damaged by fury and depressed by sadness, but the heart can adjust emotional disturbance. Therefore, diseases of the liver may be cured by the integral adjustment of the heart.

(iii) Treatment of a local disease by integral adjustment and treatment applied at another place: A local disease can be treated through the linkage between the Zang Fu, meridians, essence, Qi, and spirit. As related in the "Plain Questions": "A disease of the upper body with manifestations of reversed Qi can be cured by the application of an integral adjustment and treatment to the lower body or vice versa. At the same time, a disease in the center of the body can be cured by the application of integral treatment to the peripheral regions. The heat in patients with a febrile disease can be relieved by the administration of drugs of both cold and warm nature; and the coldness in patients with a chill disease can be eliminated by drugs with a hot and cool nature." As explained by Wang Bing, a medical scholar during the Tang Dynasty: "Why can an upper disease be cured by treatment applied to the lower part of the body? If hot drugs are administered to warm up the upper body, the cold pathogen with a tendency to rise cannot be discharged from the lower body. After the upper body is filled with a cold pathogen, hot drugs may be applied to warm up the lower body, and then the coldness in the lower body may be gradually resolved and discharged." The same explanation can be used to illustrate an upper or central disease cured by treatment applied to the lower body or peripheral parts of the body.

In TCM, early treatment without any delay is also emphasized. Bian Que (407-310 B.C.), a famous physician in the Spring and Autumn Period, traveled to Linzi, capital of the Qi State, where Qi Huangong, the king of this state, warmly hosted him. In order to repay the king's hospitality, Bian Que told him, "You have contracted an illness," because he had already examined and recognized the poor complexion of the king. "Rather than being serious, it is still just staying in the skin. However, if it is not cured in time, it will become worse." But the king did not pay attention to his advice. Five days later, Bian Que came back to visit the king and told him, "The disease has already spread to the blood vessels, and if not cured quickly, it will further worsen." But the king was unpleasant and denied suffering from any disease. Another five days passed and then Bian Que told the king, "Your disease has already arrived in the stomach and intestine, if not cured at once, it will be incurable." After his fourth visit, Bian Que left the palace quickly. When the king began to feel uncomfortable, he tried to call Bian Que back to his palace, but the physician refused, telling the messenger, "As a disease in the skin, it could be cured by decoction; after it entered the blood vessels, it could be cured by acupuncture; and after it reached the stomach and intestine, it could be cured by tincture. However, the disease of the king has now deeply invaded the bone-marrow and cannot be cured even by the God who controls the lives of human beings." The king died soon afterward as expected.

If a disease has developed to a point where it has already invaded the bone-marrow, the life of the patient is really at risk and incurable even by an extraordinary physician such as Bian Que. From this concept of "early treatment" one may draw important inspiration to promote the ecological protection movement. One day, if the non-regenerative resources of the world are completely consumed due to reckless deconstruction of the natural environment, then it will be too late to worry about the relationship between Nature and mankind. According to an epigrammatic slogan, "the last piece of water on the earth will be the drop of a human tear."

In the treatment of disease by TCM, the concept of "integral adjustment and treatment" may also be applied in the prescription of recipes. TCM physicians usually prescribe recipes with multiple herbs, although they also use single herb to treat patients on many occasions. The herbs used in TCM clinical practice are mostly vegetable in origin, although some are composed of animal organs and mineral materials. None of them produce any severe side effects. At the same time, they are regenerative natural resources with a guarantee of being continuously supplied, but without the risk of producing ecological pollution. Therefore the application of herbs to treat diseases make it easy to keep the balance of the social ecology of mankind.

2. "Prohibition Against Shooting Sleeping Birds"

In a tale recorded in the *The Analects*: In order to supply sacrificial offerings, Confucius had to capture some fish and birds, but he neither used a net made of thick cords with small meshes to catch fish nor an arrow connected to a long silk thread to shoot birds sleeping at night. This shows the kindness of Confucius toward animals. Another two important Confucians who came after him, Mencius and Xun Zi, explained further the theoretical concept of obeying natural rules and protecting the ecological environment.

(1) "Harvesting Products at an Adequate Time"

Mencius and Xun Zi emphasized again and again that in cutting trees, hunting, and fishing the productive labor should be done in a season of adequacy and prohibited during the growing stage. Mencius opposed cutting trees without any restrictions so as to protect the forest. He said, "If axes are carried into the forests on a mountain in adequate time (to cut trees), timber can be supplied without interruption."

Mencius also said, "If mulberry trees are planted on a farm of 5 *mu* (0.33 hectare), people above 50 years of age will get a silk suit to put on; if domestic animals such as chickens, pigs, and dogs are bred in time, people above 70 years of age will have meat to eat; and if crops are grown on a farm of 100 *mu* (66 hectares), a family with several members will not go hungry. If cultural education is improved in schools so as to teach people about their filial duty to their parents and respect for elders, no aged people with gray hairs will have to rush about with heavy luggage on their backs seeking a means of livelihood."

The ideology of Mencius regarding ecological protection may be summarized as follows: The resources supplied by Nature to mankind should be "eaten in a suitable time and consumed in a polite manner" in order to keep them from never being entirely used up.

In the works of Xun Zi, he repeatedly emphasized the need for people to obey the seasonal requirements of harvesting in order to obtain any natural resources. All the products acquired from Nature in the right season, such as those from mountains, forests, rivers, and lakes, should be free of taxes in order to encourage people to establish the concept of ecological protection. Therefore, "all killing (animal) and cutting (tree) labor participated in by various workers should be done according to seasonal requirements." In a discussion he provided in his work on "Popular Laws", the principles about how "to protect a suitable environment for all things of the world" were particularly emphasized. He said, "The basic social laws for the collective life of human beings are how to establish a suitable environment for all things. Then the domestic animals may grow in a regular pattern and all living things may live an expected lifespan; the domestic animals bred in an appropriate time may grow sturdily, and the trees and grass cut in an appropriate time may grow luxuriantly. If the political and educational activities of the government are arranged according to the regular changes of season, all people will work hard as one and the great men will gather together to serve and respect the government. In a society ruled by a wise leader, it will be forbidden to use axes in a forest to cut trees and grass during their growing stage so as to avoid interrupting their growth and causing their premature deaths; for the same reason, a net with small meshes and poisons are prohibited from use in catching fish, tortoises, eels, and loaches in the rivers and lakes during their reproductive period. In agricultural production, if the seasonal procedures of spring sowing, summer weeding, autumn harvesting, and winter storage can be finished in time, grains will not be in serious shortage and people may have a rich food supply. If the large ponds, deep abysses, swamps, and big rivers are closed for fishing in a regular and reasonable time, the products of fish and tortoises may be quite adequate and people may get enough income from the sale of fish for their daily lives; and if the planting and cutting of trees is arranged in accordance with the seasonal requirements, the mountains will not become barren and people will always have enough timber to use."

In addition, Xun Zi offered some suggestions about ecological protection to officials at various posts, especially his suggestion of "exploitation or prohibition according to the appropriate time" that he offered to the officials in charge of the administration of mountains, forests, and big lakes. He said, "Exploitation or prohibition to acquire wood, grass, fish, and tortoises from mountains and big lakes should be arranged accordingly, to both sufficiently fulfill the consumption needs of the country and to avoid wasting the national resources without restriction. This is their important responsibility."

In the relationship between heaven and mankind, Xun Zi held an optimistic view, and so he made a brilliant proposition. His optimism was cultivated on the basis of reasonably utilizing the natural resources and paying attention to the balance of the ecological chain in supplying enough natural resources for all. He disagreed with the concern of Mo Zi about the lack of enough resources in the world to fulfill the demands of human beings. Xun Zi believed that if people deeply respect the natural rules and pay sufficient attention to keeping balance in the ecological chain, they may certainly acquire enough material resources from Nature and therefore, "if we reasonably utilize the land for the cultivation of grain, then we may gather a rich harvest from a farm of only 1 *mu* (6.7 acres) twice a year. The fruit picked from a peach, date, or plum tree may fill several basins; the domestic and wild fowl and animals may be transported by vehicles as well as countless flying birds, such as wild ducks and wild geese; and the water products, such as fish, tortoises, eels, and loaches may be supplied in large amounts if they are permitted to grow without any interference. All living things of countless varieties, including insects, may mutually serve as foodstuffs for each other." Hence, Xun Zi set forth the prerequisite for obtaining rich material resources that is known as "benevolent administration" of the government to teach people to respect the ecological principles of Nature.

Xun Zi believed that all consumable resources on the earth are much more abundant than the actual demands of human beings, for whom, however, the fundamental requirement is to respect the growth principles of all natural living things. Then the country may accumulate enormous wealth and people may have more than enough articles for daily use. If the officials can "universally keep all things in their adequate growing condition and help them to correctly make responses to environmental changes; for example, to follow the seasonal changes of heaven; rationally obtain benefits from earth; and improve harmony among the people, then wealth may be accumulated as high as the hills and gathered as water flows from its spring to the river and sea, wave after wave... Why then should the whole country still worry about an insufficiency of wealth?"

The same concept was presented in *The Book of Rites*: "If no war happens or any funeral ceremony takes place, people may go hunting three times in the spring, autumn, and winter of each year. The hunting harvest may be used to prepare dried meat for offering sacrifices, holding a banquet for guests, and supplying the kitchen for a king. It is disrespectful to go hunting without any specific demand. Reckless hunting is devastation of Nature. When the emperor goes hunting, beasts should not be captured from all directions and an open exit should be reserved for them to escape; when dukes go hunting, the beasts should not be killed in batches. In the first lunar month, otters scatter along the river bank to capture fish as if they need them for sacrifices. Then the officials in charge of hunting affairs in the areas of mountains, lakes, and plains may allow people to go fishing over the water surface. In the ninth lunar month, jackals scatter to capture beasts as if they need them for sacrifices. Then people are allowed to go hunting in autumn. When turtledoves change to hawks, people are allowed to set nets to capture birds; after trees and grass have withered, people are allowed to go into the forest to cut trees. On the other hand, hunting by burning grass on the plain is banned while insects are still hibernating under the ground. In hunting, baby beasts and pregnant animals should not be captured or killed; the eggs of birds should not be taken away and the nests of birds should not be destroyed."

The codes of conduct in the four seasons were all stipulated in detail in *The Book of Rites*. The officials at various posts were asked to strictly follow the productive and reproductive regularities of all things in the world and the natural resources consumed by human beings had to be acquired with extreme temperance. For example, in the first month of the spring, it was banned for female birds and beasts to be offered at a sacrificial festival because, as a tradition, the Chinese people were very respectful of the growth rules for all things of the world. The forests were banned from being destroyed; it was prohibited for newborn beasts, birds just learning to fly, pregnant beasts, and young insects to be killed; the eggs of birds were not to be taken away and the nests of birds were not to be destroyed. In the first month of the spring, people were not called upon to build city walls or to be inducted into the army so as not to delay spring plowing and war was not to be initiated in this month. Otherwise, the initiator of war would certainly be punished by God. Even though war was inevitable, it should not be started from our side. Generally speaking, people should neither miss the opportune moments for production or reproduction, terminate the growth of all things, nor disturb the productive order of human beings. If the green crops on farms were destroyed by wild beasts in summer, people were permitted to drive them away, rather than kill them without restraint.

(2) "Great Men Try to Share Morality with Heaven and Earth"

A typical, ancient Chinese thought in *The Book of Changes* is the fact that the heavenly way is highly praised. At the same time, people are asked to accurately and carefully learn and emulate the active and vigorous spirit in the heavenly way so as to develop a brilliant social culture for humankind. As recorded in this book: "Heaven moves powerfully as a man, so great men should forever make efforts to improve themselves; the earth assumes itself as a woman, so great men should learn from the solidness and toughness of the earth to improve their morality and bear heavy burdens." There-fore people should learn the natural laws, namely the excellent morality with the enterprising and tolerant spirit of heaven and earth, and put these into action through unceasing efforts to improve themselves and bear any heavy burdens. In addition, the book says that the essence of natural laws is subordination, so how can people neglect the natural laws? They should always follow the natural changes and advance forward with the times.

The basic spirit in *The Book of Changes* is defined as "keeping living things alive" and continuously recreating the life of successive generations. Therefore, people should set up their administrative rules and make their plans of action according to this spirit. As an excellent concept of the "union of heaven and mankind" in Chinese traditional philosophy, this is also an inspirational idea with modern philosophical significance. This concept may fundamentally change the inorganic, mechanical concept of Nature that has developed in the Western world. At the same time, it may serve as a valu-able resource for thoughts regarding the construction of modern Chinese ecological ethics. As recorded in this book, "the so-called 'great men' al-ways keep a close link with the luster of the sun and moon, the good or bad luck of the gods and ghosts, and the morality of heaven and earth. If their actions are made in relation to the seasonal climate, heaven will not reject their requests; they should follow the natural rhythm after adjusting to the adequate climate." Generally speaking, the "great men" in *The Book of Changes* are people who can skillfully comprehend and strictly obey the ba-sic spirit and human society. If these under their control, they will certainly respect and obey the ecological principles.

According to the "Philosophy of Changes," the complicated processes of natural changes should be carefully watched and followed by people in guiding their actions, so the concept of the "union of heaven and mankind" is outlined in the book. In the practice of the basic spirit to obtain real bene-fits for mankind, people must make earnest efforts, rather than passively adapt to the natural changes. As said in *The Book of Changes*, "The creators of *The Book of Changes* watch the brightness of sun, moon, and stars with their chins up and examine the configuration of mountains, rivers, and plains with their heads bowed. Therefore, they thoroughly understand the apparent and hidden natural principles. In addition, they understand the objective laws of life and death because they can follow the development of all things from beginning to end. They understand the activities of gods and ghosts because they can examine the coagulation of Qi to form a body and the dispersal of Qi into a soul." This book thoroughly expounds the laws of the movement of heaven and earth, so the creators never make objection to these laws. They understand everything in the world and teach people to correct their faults with morality so that they can do anything without fault. As for managing any activities, the creators have never looked worried or pessimistic because they are aware of the natural laws and lack any decadent desires. They are universally fond of all the people in the world because they are always very kind, honest, and loyal in taking care of the natural environment. Therefore, the 'Philosophy of Changes' is as capacious as a container, capable of keeping all growing matters in it without being neglected. This can help everything to eventually show its presence in the world without anything being missed. Thus the creators understand the changes of day and night as a superb wisdom. Therefore, *The Book of Changes* can illustrate all changes without fixed patterns because all things in the world are quite mysterious and concealed without definite shape."

The theories of the "Philosophy of Changes" are broad and deep, showing the configuration of heaven and earth as well as the rules of their movement. As explained in *The Book of Changes*: "As a Yang trigram, the 'Qian' of hard nature is concentrated and contracted while in a static stage, but it is unbendingly rigid in a dynamic stage; and as a Yin trigram, the 'Kun' of soft nature is closed and hidden while in a static stage, but it is opened and spread in a dynamic stage." This book further says that "the hard, huge, wide, and soft nature of the 'Philosophy of Changes' is comparable with that of heaven and earth; the nature of free change in the Philosophy without any retardation is similar to that of the four seasons; the nature of soft Yin and hard Yang in the philosophy is coincident with that of sun and moon; and the perfection of the simple and common ideology in the philosophy is identical to that of supreme morality."

Heaven and earth in the "Philosophy of Changes" are always regarded as examples for the actions of human beings. Therefore, in the "activities" of human beings in reforming and utilizing Nature, people must exploit Nature temperately rather than violently, while at the same time, the rational demands of human beings, namely the subjective request to receive service from Nature, should be actively raised with "sincerity and faith." Then the demands of human beings may be fit for the functioning laws of heaven and earth and the relationship between mankind and Nature may be developed to the highest standard. As recorded in this book: "The 'Philosophy of Changes' raises four requirements for great men, exquisite diction for writers and speakers; flexibility of action for clerks in charge of general affairs; wonderful artistry for manufacturers of tools; and accurate prediction for wizards. Therefore, great men may raise their questions of the 'Philosophy of Changes' by words to receive prompt answers before they begin to put their thoughts into action, no matter how remote, nearby, hidden, or profound the questions may be! If they are not raised by the most sincere and faithful people, how can they accomplish such state of mind? The changes in Nature can be repeatedly studied by complex deduction with yarrow grass, which can show the changing graces of heaven and earth as well as the changing configuration of all things in the world."

The verb "xiang" in this Philosophy means "to imitate." It is not to simply imitate the visible superficial appearance of all things in the world, but the spirit inside their body, namely their vivid spiritual status of their life. As mentioned in this book: "The word 'xiang' in this Philosophy is used to define the invisible laws found by great men, imitate them with visible configuration, and symbolize the appropriate environment for some particular things."

In this Philosophy, various phenomena shown by the heaven and earth together with their movement are known as "faxiang." As mentioned in this book: "There is no other 'faxiang' more mighty than that of heaven and earth; no other change more smooth than the change of four seasons; no more 'Xuanxiang' more bright than the shiny sun and moon; …Therefore, all miraculous things are created by heaven, so great men try to learn from them; the symbols of good or bad luck are shown by heaven, so great men try to copy them; and the painting of the dragon is drawn in the region of the Yellow River and the ancient Chinese characters are carved on tortoise shells in the region of the Luohe River, so great men try to make 'Eight Trigrams' to imitate them."

In addition to the apparent activities of heaven and earth, their spiritual phenomena should also be imitated according to the theory about formation of the universe in the "Philosophy of Changes." As said in the "Preliminary Trigrams": "Following the formation of heaven and earth appeared men and women, husbands and wives, fathers and sons, emperors and ministers, and officials of high and low ranks in succession, and the regulations about ceremony and propriety among people of different generations and ranks were finally established." Human society with its civilization is derived from Nature. Therefore, how can people sever the intimate link between human beings and the universe and all things in the world, while at the same time refusing to show respect for and fear of Nature? The "Philosophy of Changes" has left a deep influence on the Chinese people in traditional society; they always kept an attitude of respect and fear of Nature and believed that Nature was just as alive as human beings.

During the Song Dynasty, the belief in the "love to relatives, ordinary people, and all things" from the ancient Confucians was modified by the new Confucians as a "union of kind people with the universe and all things in the world." This new development of ecological ethics was an inheritance from the original humane and religious thought. As recorded in a book of philosopher Zhang Zai (1020-1077): "The Qian trigrams may be regarded as the father of mankind and the Kun trigrams as the mother of them; a person is only a minute and ignorant individual in the universe. Therefore, the whole entity of heaven and earth is also the foundation of human beings and its spirit is the wisdom and morality of human beings. All people are our brothers and all things are our friends." Zhang Zai added, "Nothing can exist alone. Without mutual competence or service, extension or bending, and separation or union between all things in the world, nothing can acquire its own specific nature, although it may grow up to assume its shape." This concept was further expounded by Wang Fuzhi: "As making an analogical comparison, the existence of one thing must yield benefit to another." Zhang Zai asked people to be open-minded so as to enjoy the close relationship between all things. He said, "Examine all things in the world with an open mind. If one of them is neglected, there may be a corner in one's heart not filled with passion. For ordinary people, their narrow minds are only filled with ordinary trivial matters, which do not bias the minds of great men. They always regard all things in the world as being as lovely as themselves."

All the ideas of the above-mentioned philosophers reflect the traditional attitude of the Chinese people in their respect of Nature. Therefore, with restriction, they frugally utilize the natural resources for longstanding and persistent consumption. This traditional concept with a long history may produce an important influence on the contemporary Chinese people. In the modernization of China, the Chinese people must be soberly aware of the importance of protecting the environment according to our traditional culture. In order to meet the competition of energy resources in the contemporary international society, we must actively exploit and frugally consume our natural resources.

3. "The Highest Good Is Like That of Water"

Among the traditional Chinese philosophies, Taoism paid much more attention to respect for the natural laws. The Taoists tried their best to learn from Nature. The essence of Taoism is to learn the practical laws of Nature and to apply these in the administration of human society for the maintenance of harmony between mankind and Nature. Of course, Taoism also showed its defect in the neglect of the application of natural laws for the lives of human beings. As criticized by Xun Zi: The thought of Zhuang Zi is "to pay attention merely to heaven, but to forget human beings themselves." This means that Zhuang Zi only asked people to follow the natural laws, but he forgot to encourage people to make dynamic efforts for their own benefit. However, people in contemporary society have become quite arrogant toward Nature because of their advanced science and technology. Therefore, it may be helpful to them, if they listen attentively to the wise advice of Taoism, to maintain a reasonable relationship toward mankind and Nature.

(1) Taoism Follows Nature

Lao Zi, the founder of Taoism, had some different thoughts from that of Confucius. Confucius tried his best to recover the kindness of humanity, while at the same time supplementing and standardizing humanity through ceremonies and propriety. On the other hand, Lao Zi tried his best to break down the superstition toward gods and ghosts while asking people to obey the objective Way (or heavenly way) so as to keep human society stable and orderly. Lao Zi believed that in general the laws of human affairs must match those of heavenly actions, known as the "sharing of laws between heaven and mankind." This acted as a philosophical theory to support the concept about the duty of human beings to respect Nature for their survival.

Lao Zi believed that heaven and earth do not purposely pursue longevity, but they may live for a long time. This indicates that Lao Zi just wanted to teach people, especially the rulers, not to purposely pursue longevity. A wise ruler should act like water, because this always provides benefits to all things rather than stirring up conflict between them. The people most familiar with Taoism always humbly get along with others.

There were only about five thousand Chinese characters used to write the book *Lao Zi* (《老子》), in which this concept was expressed in several places: People should support all things to grow naturally, but not possess them or brag about the deeds they do for them; at the same time, take care of them, but not wantonly use them for their own good.

Lao Zi also praised great men. However, the great men in his criteria were ones able to receive and bear with all people and things in the world. Therefore, he said, "Great men often secure people, so no person will be useless; and secure things, so nothing will be discarded as garbage." The garbage produced in such huge quantities by modern society is really troublesome to human beings nowadays. The recycling of resources may be regarded as a standard by which to evaluate the efforts made by human beings in environmental protection and the strictness of this standard should be gradually advanced in coming years. Lao Zi believed that the ideal society administered by great men should be absolutely environmentally protective, with people neither idle nor wasting anything. Therefore, the thoughts of Lao Zi may serve as a useful inspiration to modern society. In general, the thoughts of Lao Zi are misunderstood as "doing nothing," when actually there are "many things to do." However, no matter what should be done, it should be done in accordance with the natural laws. Great men also manage and utilize all things according to their own nature and regularity, rather than according to subjective human desires. "Specific objects are produced after the Way is dissociated. Great men use such objects according to their properties and assign people to administer them. Therefore the wisest administration will not separate such properties from them."

The "Great Way" of Lao Zi is the general administrator of everything growing up naturally, freely, and comfortably. He said, "The Great Way may flow to either the left or right side. It does not refuse to help anything grow up, but will not owe up the merits to itself; it enjoys success in helping the growth of all things, but will not control them. Because of the lack of any desire, it may be considered as something quite small; on the other hand, it gathers all things around it, but will not control them, so it may also be considered as something quite big, although it does not think so itself. On the contrary, it is really very great."

As for reformation in Nature, if people follow the ideology of Lao Zi in respect to natural laws, Nature will provide wealth and a comfortable environment to improve human life. If the natural resources are taken over from Nature by human beings with care rather than by violence, the relationship between Nature and mankind will be mutually dependent instead of being suppressed.

(2) Zhuang Zi's Thought of Respect for "Material Nature"

Zhuang Zi, an outstanding disciple of Lao Zi, followed and developed the thoughts of Lao Zi. In his theory about the "relationship between heaven and mankind," he particularly emphasized the difference between heaven and human beings. He said, "As a supreme comprehension, people should know what can be done by heaven and what can be done by human beings themselves. If they know what can be done by heaven, it may help them live forever; if they know what can be done by human beings, they may get new knowledge and prolong their life span without premature death. This is the supreme standard of knowledge." Here, the word "heaven" used by Zhuang Zi is "Nature" in the modern concept, and the term "human beings" is used universally for all people at any time.

Zhuang Zi paid much respect to "material nature," which for him was the internal regularity of a substance. He believed that everything is reasonable if it is natural, and he said, "The legs of wild ducks are short. They will be very troublesome if you try to elongate their legs. Similarly, the legs of cranes are long. They will be very sad if you cut their legs short." Therefore, in dealing with the relationship between Nature and human beings, people should keep their minds clear and not rack their brains to alter the proper nature of a substance in vain. As for facing Nature, the best attitude for people to adopt is to respect the "material nature."

We cannot find any statement about protection of the environment in the philosophy of Zhuang Zi, but from both his opposition and support of compliance with the internal nature of all things we may reasonably draw out an idea of his concept against exaggerated artificiality and modernization.

Zhuang Zi

Zhuang Zi believed that all riots were caused by rulers who were keen on conquering Nature but ignored how to live in a noble way. Why? He made this explanation: When you see birds flying wildly about all day long with anxiety, it is because the knowledge of how to produce a bow and arrow is much advanced; when you see fish swimming violently in the water without any calmness, it is because the knowledge of how to produce a fish net and fish hook is much advanced; and when you see beasts running madly in the mountain and forest without taking a breathing spell, it is because the knowledge of how to produce instruments and nets to capture them is much advanced.

Zhuang Zi criticized people who only sought knowledge of how to obtain all things from Nature and neglected the well-known knowledge how to obtain luck, people who only remembered to fight against the evils recognized by them and forgot to re-examine their false virtue, which was considered as true virtue by them and resulted in there being a disturbed prospect in front of them. The brightness of the sun and moon in the sky was sheltered; the essence of the mountains and rivers on earth was destroyed; and the change of the seasonal climate was interrupted. All organisms, including birds with wings in the sky and worms with soft bodies on the ground might lose their internal nature. All of these disturbances were caused by people who wanted to conquer material nature to the extreme!

Zhuang Zi repeatedly criticized those people who kept birds in bird-cages, drove oxen and horses with reins, and deprived all things of their freedom just for their own satisfaction. He always appealed to people to keep material nature intact. A tale in his book *Zhuang Zi* may be used to express his position. One day, the King of Lu State obtained a miraculous bird in the suburbs and kept it with respect in the temple. The bird became dull and sad. A meal of whole ox or sheep was served to the bird with holy music being played to improve its appetite. However, the bird did not eat or drink anything and eventually died three days later. Zhuang Zi said in regard to this tale, "The bird died because it was fed with the favorable tastes of human beings instead of that of the bird itself. A bird should be allowed to stay in the forest; fly over the land, rivers, and lakes; catch loaches and small fish as its food, and freely come and go in the loose company of its own kind."

According to the viewpoint of the contemporary people, this fable was used by Zhuang Zi to explain the mutually transforming relationship between inorganic, organic, and biological matters with human beings. He said, "Among the various species, there is a microorganism which propagates in water. It becomes moss on the water margin and becomes plantain on the highlands. The plantain becomes water plantain, the root of which becomes the larva of the dung-beetle and the leaf of which becomes the butterfly. Soon afterwards, the butterfly becomes an insect in a moulted form by the name of *quduo*, which lives under the stove. In a thousand days the *quduo* becomes a bird by the name of *ganyugu*, whose saliva in turn becomes an insect by the name of *simi*, which again in turn becomes another insect by the name of *jiuyou*; the insect by the name of *maorui* is born from the insect by the name of *fuquan*. The *yangxi* grass lives with the bamboo that no longer sprouts, which gives birth to an insect by the name of *qingning*, which in turn gives birth to the leopard, and which again in turn gives birth to the horse, which again in turn gives birth to the man. The man, in his turn, reverts to the microorganism. Everything in the world comes out of a microorganism and goes back to it." This is the concept of Zhuang Zi about the "transformation of things," although he had no knowledge about the relationship between inorganic and organic substances nor between plants and animals in a sense of modern chemistry and biology. As said by him: "All things may be transformed in shape." In the chapter "On the Uniformity of All Things" of *Zhuang Zi*, there is an interesting tale, which goes like this: "I, by the name of Zhuang Zhou, once dreamed that I was a butterfly, a butterfly fluttering happily here and there. I was so pleased that I forgot that I was Zhuang Zhou. When I suddenly woke up, I was astonished to find that I was as a matter of fact Zhuang Zhou. Did Zhuang Zhou dream of the butterfly or did the butterfly dream of Zhuang Zhou? Between Zhuang Zhou and the butterfuly there must be some distinctions. This is called 'the transformation of things'."

As a representative of Taoism, Zhuang Zi revealed the internal linkage between mankind and Nature. With a wonderful imagination, he wrote suggestive poetry about the organic ecological ideology, and produced a profound influence on the literature and arts of the following dynasties. The concept of praising Nature is especially valuable today when the materialism of the industrial age is prevailing and Nature is regarded as something passive and spiritless.

Nevertheless, the modified theory of the "union of heaven and mankind" does not advocate that people passively follow the rules of Nature but, instead, that they actively promote heavenly way by human laws and make use of heavenly way to serve human laws. This is the difference between the ancient and modern ideology of environmental protection and ecological ethics.

4. To Conduct Heavenly Way by Human Laws

The philosophic thoughts of Wang Fuzhi, one of the most important thinkers in the latter period of ancient China, are extensive and profound. He developed a unique viewpoint about the relationship between human beings and heaven from the traditional ideology found in the ancient classics. In addition to giving respect to the natural laws, he also asked people to distinguish human laws from natural laws so that both might fully play a dynamic role in the creation and development of the brilliant civilization of human beings. Therefore, his theory of a "union of heavenly way and human laws" may be regarded as a forecast of the spontaneous change from the ancient traditional society to the contemporary modern society of China.

(1) Heaven as a Tool and Human Beings as the Executors of the Laws

In the philosophical thought of Wang Fuzhi, heaven, the common concept of the universe in Chinese traditional philosophy and culture, was precisely analyzed and divided into five grades. The first grade, "heaven of heaven," is in charge of the "union of human beings and materials" that promotes the transformation of things; the second grade, "heaven of materials," is what belongs to materials; the third grade, "heaven of human beings," is what belongs to people; the fourth grade, "heaven of oneself," is what belongs to a few outstanding persons; and the fifth grade, "heaven of mass," is what belongs to the vast number of common people.

Among the five grades of heaven, Wang Fuzhi showed special respect toward the "heaven of heaven" and "heaven of materials," because they were closely related to his ecological philosophy. He said, "Great men take advantage from heaven because they want to fulfill the objective social demands of the common population. They never adjust and change public opinion about social demands to their own standpoint, so they never waste the natural resources provided by heaven, and the materials may be distinguished from each other. They never overstep the authority of heaven so that people may live in peace and contentment no matter where they settle." When the natural properties of human beings and materials are under the control of heaven, people may live anywhere peacefully and safely and their customs and habits may become pure and honest after education. In reforming and utilizing natural resources, people should follow the laws of heaven and properties of all natural things because these only provide service to kind and honest people. It is very useful to improve their customs and habits.

When distinguishing the thoughts of ancient Confucianism and Taoism regarding the concept of the "union of heavenly way and human laws," Wang Fuzhi particularly emphasized the need to reasonably apply the heavenly way rather than passively follow them and allow the people to be ordered about by them. People should give respect to the "heaven of heaven" and "heaven of material," but this does not mean that people must absolutely follow them at every step. Therefore, he said, "From remote ancient times, people never understood how Nature produces its influence on human beings; at the same time, the skillful techniques of Nature can never be modified by the reforming efforts of human beings. Heaven scatters honesty and justice over the world and people must make an effort to practice these virtues in their behaviors. All things in Nature can be divided into the *Yin* and *Yang* categories and people may show their kindness and brotherhood in correspondence; there are five permanent stars in the sky and people have five sense organs in correspondence. However, heaven and the human body are physically and substantially different from each other so they cannot be united together.... Heaven and human beings are different both in shape and nature, so all that people can learn from heaven are its laws."

Therefore, in the viewpoint of Wang Fuzhi, a correct relationship may be maintained between heaven and mankind by the practice of following the practical laws of heaven. But the heavenly way should not be blindly applied in managing the social activities of human beings. People should play a role in achieving their target for a better life through their own efforts rather than through the help of great men. This is the basic difference of life style between human beings and animals. According to Wang Fuzhi: "The laws of human society are only a fraction of the heavenly way so that people should not simply take over the latter in applying the way of human society itself. If the important responsibility in supporting and assisting Nature is only assigned to great men, this is certainly wrong because it is just like allowing Nature to act willfully. The swimming of fish and flying of birds are all activities that allow Nature to act willfully. If people do not dare to regard themselves as great men and support and assist Nature in achieving the goal of human beings for a better life, how can they avoid acting as animals being passively controlled by Nature?"

In the management of human society, Wang Fuzhi strongly opposed the concept of "determination by heaven." He believed that people are able to modify certain natural phenomena if they can follow the natural laws exactly. For example, people may produce some new instruments for themselves to improve their material and spiritual life although heaven has never prepared these for human beings. Such creativity of human beings is acquired from the rational social regimen, valuable culture, and traditions of human beings, as well as the practice of heavenly way that show the brightness of humanity. As affirmed by Wang Fuzhi: "If people only follow the heavenly way without any creation by themselves, how can they be regarded as human beings? Any troubles produced by 'assisting heaven' to do something are no more terrible than those caused by always being determined by heaven."

Wang Fuzhi made a brilliant proposition: "Heaven is the tool and human beings are the executors of the laws" about the relationship between heaven and humankind because he put so much emphasis on the unique property of human laws. If people can rationally handle the heavenly way, then heaven may be regarded as an ideal tool to be used to show the dignity of human laws. Xun Zi never regarded heaven as a big tool, although he had the concept: "Control the heavenly way and apply it." Therefore, we may come to the conclusion that the proposition of "heaven as a tool and human beings as the executors of the laws" is not found in the traditional conceptions of Confucianism and Taoism. According to Wang Fuzhi: "It is common sense to consider heaven as the source of abstract laws and human beings as the practical tools, but without great wisdom how can people understand such an important truth as to consider 'heaven the tool and human beings as the executors of the laws?'…If human laws can be widely applied, then heaven can be managed, the earth can be controlled, and all things in the world can be finally designed and produced without any trace of artificial processing. Therefore, we may claim: 'heaven as a tool and human beings as the executors of the laws'."

(2) "To Conduct Heavenly Way by Human Laws"

Wang Fuzhi clearly developed the concept of "conducting heavenly way by human laws" from the traditional thought of the "union of heavenly way and human laws." This meant making use of the heavenly way for the benefit of people according to their demands. Therefore, the concept of "heaven as a tool and human beings as the executors of the laws" does not allow people to uncontrollably and violently consume the natural resources. Wang Fuzhi believed that the "human laws" used to conduct the heavenly way are laws derived from the heavenly way itself, and so he said, "The basic social laws of human beings are developed on the basis of 'benevolence' and 'righteousness,' so the guidance of heavenly way by human laws is a matter of managing human affairs according to the demands of benevolence and righteousness. If people only occasionally act in keeping with benevolence and righteousness under heavenly promotion, one actually cannot differentiate the behavior of human beings from that of animals." However, if people can keep faithfulness to their king, just as bees and ants do in fulfilling their filial duty to their parents or as sheep and birds do, they are no different from animals and how then do they show the brilliant luster of humanity? To the statement of Zhang Zai: "Our body is filled with the Qi of heaven and earth," Wang Fuzhi provided a new explanation by saying, "The substantial material (Qi) of heaven and earth is used to fill up and build our body, however, our body does not necessarily have to make full use of such material. Heaven and earth have kindly provided all things to people for consumption, but people do not have to treat them with benevolence used towards people. After the morality of human beings derived from the spirit of heaven and earth has been established in the human body, it may play a role in producing the various functions of human laws through concentrating the human mind and promoting their desire to achieve a high tide. Following this, the spirit of heaven and earth no longer produces any effect on human morality. The emotions, such as joy, sadness, and happiness, must be betrayed after careful consideration and the decision over one's life as a means of producing human laws should not be made without hesitation."

As mentioned above, Zhuang Zi particularly emphasized the need to absolutely obey the heavenly way of the "separation of mankind from heaven," but Wang Fuzhi cast more emphasis on the rational utilization of natural resources by people according to their demands. People can never treat all things as well as taking care of human beings themselves. This is impossible even for vegetarians. The basic concept of ecological protectionism is intended to acquire and utilize natural resources in conformation with the heavenly way. However, the rational concept of protectionism should contain information on how to clearly understand the limitations of human power and the infiniteness of natural power and to reasonably utilize natural resources with respect to heavenly way. The principle of the humanity of human beings, different from that of animals, is how to recognize the beauty of wisdom and virtue of internal morality, as well as how to escape from the control of blind natural forces, instead of being a way to seize more natural resources for the enjoyment of a luxurious life. Therefore, the concept of Wang Fuzhi "to conduct heavenly way by human laws" may have active significance and provide an inspiration for the development of modern ecological ethics.

The Great Wall, a Model of the Idea of Defensive Strategy, Witness to China's Peaceful Development

The pattern of civilization in any society is the result of the subjective construction of its people, instead of a selection of Nature. The future development of humankind cannot be completely guaranteed, but the exploration and discovery of cultural resources related to peaceful coexistence among different countries may play a positive role in choosing and adjusting the political line of politicians in the administration of their country.

In the modern world, a deep concern over the sovereignty of a country may serve to stimulate military competition among the big economic and political nations over a long historical period, because the maintenance of dignity for a sovereign country may rely on powerful military force and rich comprehensive national strength. As a big country with a wide territory, a vast population, and a longstanding cultural tradition, China has become a large sovereign country that has quickly developed along with other modern nations. However, different from the nations on the European and American continents, the Confucian philosophical view in China that was gradually established since the Qin and Han dynasties already occupies a dominant position in Chinese society and exercises an important influence in contemporary China, although its position has been taken over by Marxism. The Silk Road is a witness to the history of peaceful economic and cultural communication among countries and nationalities of the world. Confucianism

The Great Wall represents the defensive strategy of the ancient Chinese people.

particularly emphasizes the application of a "moral ruling policy" to manage domestic and foreign affairs. Therefore, China will not export its cultural ideology by means of military force, even though the Chinese economy will continue its rapid development during the next several years. The Chinese people will choose a political line of pluralistic and peaceful development according to their traditional cultural spirit: to "valuing harmony," "respect morality," and "harmony with differences." As a model of the Chinese national ideology, the Great Wall represents the defensive strategy of China.

1. Analyzing the Ideology of the Great Wall as a Defensive Strategy

The Great Wall was considered a symbol of sadness by the common people of China in ancient times. The *Crying Indictment of Ms. Mengjiang*

Against the Great Wall is a folk song directed against the construction of Great Wall by Qin Shi Huang (first emperor of the Qin Dynasty, 246-209 B.C.). "In the first lunar month, the red lamps are hung house by house to celebrate the New Year. Other couples are sleeping in the same bed, but my husband went away to build the Great Wall." It is an indictment with deep hatred that condemns the tyranny of Qin Shi Huang in causing the separation of a couple unable to enjoy the happiness of a new marriage during the Chinese New Year.

In fact, the construction of the Great Wall was neither started by Qin Shi Huang nor ended by him. During the Warring States Period, the Zhao and Yang states had already built up their own Great Walls to provide a barrier against the Hun. After the union of all the states under Qin Shi Huang, the isolated walls were linked together as a huge military barrier to effectively prevent an invasion by the Hun. It was reconstructed even in the Ming Dynasty.

Actually the Great Wall could not play a significant role in preventing an invasion from the north. On the contrary, it was the strong military force of the empires of the following dynasties that kept the Hun invaders far away from the northern boundary of China. The famous General Bai Qi of the Qin Dynasty won a war against the Huns and entered their land for a long distance. During the Han Dynasty, the generals Wei Qing and Huo Qubing brought more than several hundred thousand soldiers to fight the Huns and drive them out of the desert area. Since then, the northern boundary has remained peaceful and calm for over hundreds of years.

Putting the historical stories aside, as regards to the relationship between different nationalities, the Great Wall may serve as a model in demonstrating the strategic thought of the ancient Chinese people – the ideology of defensive strategy that produced a deep influence on Chinese society during the dynasties following the Qin and Han dynasties. All the states ruled by the Zhou Empire were superior in terms of civilization and agricultural production to the regions occupied by minority nationalities far from the central area of the Empire. States with agriculture as their chief form of economic production demanded both enough labor force and a stable political and social environment to secure their agricultural production. In such a society, people were neither skilled at a fast-moving war, nor able to bear attacks and sufferings of war. The "governance with virtue" established during the Zhou Dynasty produced an important influence on the politicians of the following dynasties, so they applied the policy of conciliation to the minority nationalities and ruled them with benevolence. Another reason for the application of such a policy to these minorities was the infertility of their land, which was neither fit for agricultural production nor worthy of occupation. Due to the political, economic, cultural, and geographic reasons listed above, the politicians of the dynasties following the Qin and Han always maintained a defensive strategy in order to maintain the peace and safety of their country. Throughout Chinese history the application of this policy has been basically effective and successful in promoting the development of the economy and keeping the cultural prosperity of China.

After the Mongolian people seized power from the Southern Song Dynasty and the Manchurian people conquered the Ming Dynasty, both eventually adopted the cultural tradition and political regimen of the Han nationality and thus accomplished a cultural mixture through a complicated course. At the same time, the cultural influence of Chinese people in loving peace has spread widely.

The Chinese people regard the Great Wall as a model in showing their defensive strategy, instead of a closure of their country's gate and a refusal to link with the outside world. The Silk Road and Zheng He's seven oceanic voyages indicate that the Chinese people love peace and prefer to make economic and cultural contacts with other peoples. In other words, the Chinese people have a sincere desire to carry on peaceful communications

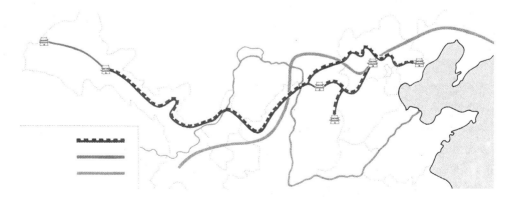

Sketch map of the Great Wall

193

rather than a drive to undergo expansion of their civilization. Therefore, the defensive strategy is a characteristic view of the peace-loving Chinese people.

There is no way to deny the fact that since the 18th century the ideology of a defensive strategy has gradually exposed its weakness. After modern capitalistic society rose in prominence, China several times lost its chance to achieve a simultaneous development with the Western world. The defects of this strategy were clearly exposed during the Opium War of 1840. After that the Chinese people began to learn from the Westerners.

From the viewpoint of international relationships, the Chinese traditional ideology is valuable in keeping peace; however from the standpoint of this country itself, it hindered and delayed the further development of China for a long time.

2. "Valuing Harmony," "Harmony with Differences" and the Independent Foreign Policy of Peace

As a matter of historical fact, during the prosperous and powerful stage of ancient China, for example the times when it was ruled by Wu (140-86 B.C.) of the Han Dynasty and Taizong (627-650) of the Tang Dynasty, the emperors did make war on surrounding countries. However, in the long years of Chinese history, China's relations with those countries were peaceful. The methods of "*jimi*," "presenting tributes to the emperor," as well as the policy of "peace through marriage" that were applied by China may clearly show the peaceful attitude toward managing relations between the different countries. Even though the Chinese economy has achieved rapid development in recent years, China still favors the policy of "valuing harmony" and joint development with foreign countries rather than a policy of treating neighboring countries as the enemy or as a barrier. The concept of "valuing harmony" of the Chinese people will certainly result in the Chinese government adopting a comparatively mild manner in the management of international relations and the treatment of conflicts between races and countries. In general, the Chinese cultural tradition may prevent their politicians from getting benefits for their own country by willfully neglecting benefits to other countries. On the contrary, Chinese politicians are encouraged to try their best to equally and comprehensively think about the balance of benefits between different countries. Therefore, the Chinese people will most likely choose peaceful development instead of outward expansion as their developing policy because of the traditional values in their civilization.

As a country with a longstanding cultural and historical tradition, China will follow the philosophy of "harmony with differences" of Confucianism, so it will always adopt an independent and self-determinant foreign policy, and treat various international affairs with a prerequisite of mutual respectfulness and harmony, without blind dictation for others. Both the international and domestic political activities are practiced with wisdom and experience. Therefore, politicians must be equipped not only with a rational political ideology but also with rich political wisdom and experiences in order to intelligently and indomitably realize their goal. The political intelligence gradually accumulated through political practice over the longstanding historical period and used to administer a country with such a huge territory must be a valuable characteristic, hard to obtain and valuable to people both in China and countries all over the world.

In China, modernization must be realized according to the actual national and social conditions that are different from those of the Western countries. Today Chinese officials and scholars repeatedly emphasize the construction of a modernized country with a specific Chinese pattern. It is not only a political slogan but also the practice of tradition: "valuing harmony" and "harmony with differences."

3. Ideology of "Great Harmony" and the Peace-loving World Outlook of the Chinese People

The ideal society of Taoism as "a small country with a small population" is not a popular Chinese political concept, although it is still affixed with some significance in the modern world. In the traditional Chinese culture, the popular concept of an ideal society is called "Great Harmony" of equality and peacefulness, which may serve as an internal restraint in Chinese society and joins the competition for benefits with an ordinary and rational spiritual attitude.

The typical statement about the concept of "Great Harmony" was first recorded in the Confucian classic, *The Book of Rites*. As a basic conception of this idea, the author wrote, "The world is a community with great men selected to administer it with honesty and harmony." Until the 19th century, Kang Youwei (1858-1927), a great reformist thinker, provided an illustration of this concept in his *Great Commonwealth* (《大同书》) as the beautiful hope for an ideal society held by Chinese people in the early stage of the modern era.

After a study of the history of the wars between different countries and races in both China and Western countries, Kang Youwei wrote of the harmfulness of war. He talked about the inevitability of war as due to the selfishness of people and foretold the possibility of star wars. He said, "The assemblage of people from separation and the exploitation of land from barrenness are a natural development of heavenly and human affairs." After "the land is opened to travel," the establishment of a single country may be an interesting development of the globe. If traffic between the stars can be established, there may be endless merger of stars and those stars may eventually unite together. But in the process of the union of stars, war is inevitable, and always brings disaster to people. Mankind may not be able to watch such a star war. However, the suffering of mankind caused by wars between different countries is today a matter of reality. He said, "After the establishment of countries in the world, the people in one country will plunder other countries in the name of benefits for their own country until nothing is left in the defeated country." Therefore, he believed that the existence of different countries is the original source of wars and all countries must be destroyed in order to relieve the sufferings of mankind.

As a new reformist Confucian in modern China and in distinction from traditional Confucianism, he regarded the present countries in the world as a crime against the will of the people. Therefore, he suggested abolishing military troops and boundaries between countries in order to relieve the people's sufferings that are caused by the collective life controlled by their countries.

In a Constitution designed by Kang Youwei for the "Great Harmonious

World," he combined the cultural traditions of various countries and the principle of equality of modern democratic politics. He said in his Constitution, "People are all supplied by the public without taxes; people commit no crime and everyone enjoys public rights; and all are equal without trade. There is no discrimination between sexes or races. All people are equal because there are no countries, slaves, or penal servitude. Respect is offered to all schools of ancient and modern philosophies, all religions and doctrines, ancient philosophers and other personal gods, rather than to heaven alone."

Tan Sitong (1865-1898), one of seven leaders of the Wuxu Reform Movement in 1898, also presented an ideology of Great Harmony of his own, although he did not write any book about his concept. He provided a new explanation about the "benevolence" of Confucianism and regarded "union" as the most important significance of "benevolence," for example, the "union between China and foreign countries" means that "all countries, no matter far away or nearby, big or small, are considered to be one single unit in a peaceful world." In this outlook, "peace" and "Great Harmony" were particularly emphasized. Much as in Christianity, he deemed, "The establishment of a religion is not only for people in one country to worship, but also for those in many other countries no matter whether they are wise or foolish. To seek benefits for people of one's own country should not ruin the interest of people in other countries. Rather it is better to share benefits with others." The "Axiom of All Nations" proposed by Tan Sitong contains the basic principles of modern international laws and ethics. He said, "The administration of our globe is better if we treat the world as a whole without differences between countries." Tan Sitong, in providing a new explanation for Zhuang Zi's statement "I have heard of letting the world be and letting the world alone, but I have never heard of governing the world," said, "The administration of a country means the presence of a country, but the liberation of a country means the absence of a country.... If all people are free, they no longer belong to any country, and if there is no country, the boundaries will have disappeared, wars will have ceased, suspicion will be cleared, tactics will be discarded, differences among people will be abolished, and only equality will be present. The country is seemingly existent, but actually not. After the emperor is dethroned, the differences between people of high and low social strata will disappear; if justice can be upheld, the differences between rich and poor people will no more be present." Finally he simplified his concept as being "an area within thousands of miles in which there is only 'one family' or 'one person'."

Tan Sitong also borrowed a concept from Buddhism to bolster his position: "All people will be promoted to Buddhas." Then there will not be any Buddha, even no religion itself; there will be neither monarchic nor democratic politics, and finally all restrictions to the globe, even to the universe, will be removed.

This is a radical proposition in the ideology of "Great Harmonious World" promoted to its extreme. Later on, Mao Zedong, one of the leaders of the first generation of the Chinese Communist Party, wrote this sentence: "In a peaceful world with the same coolness and warmth all over the globe" in one of his poems to express his yearning for that world.

The history of modern China shows that equality among people or countries has been particularly emphasized by the Chinese through the presentation of the "Great Harmony" concept from Kang Youwei to the establishment of the People's Republic of China as a socialist country. Both are closely related to each other. Up to the present, the People's Republic of China has paid attention all along to keeping "equality with countries no matter how big or small they may be" in the management of international relationships. Therefore, China has established equal diplomatic relationships with many less-developed countries. This is consistent with the Chinese political and cultural tradition: "The world is of one family."

4. Application of Moral Politics and Establishing a Peaceful International Political Order

The application of "governance with virtue" is an ancient cultural concept in China. In the ancient classic book, *Collection of Ancient Texts*, the "governance with virtue" applied by Yao and Shun, two great emperors in remote antiquity, was recorded as a model. The clear idea of "governance with virtue" was first advocated by Confucius, a representative of Chinese civilization, in order to help the kings of the various states of the Zhou

Dynasty apply a system of politics for the establishment of a harmonious political character. In application of this political concept for modern sovereign countries, the word "virtue" may be described as modern humanitarianism. Contrary to public opinion, Confucius warmly praised Guan Zhong, a great politician of Qi State, because he adopted a non-military strategy to unite other states in making common efforts in support of the Zhou Empire. Confucius praised him for: "Joining with other kings nine times without use of force." What a great political activity with benevolence and virtue that was!

In the late Spring and Autumn Period, the kings of the various states often fomented unjust wars to seize the people and land of other states. Confucius was quite resentful of this chaotic political situation. He extolled "governance with virtue" with a poetic description: "If a state applies 'governance with virtue,' it is like the Polaris shining in the high sky and surrounded by many circulating stars." At present, in the management of international relationships, if a big civilized country does not compel other countries through military force to change their political regimen, this may help the people of other countries to improve their lives through normal economic cooperation and trade. It may also prompt other countries to adjust their political formation and lifestyle through the peaceful exchange of cultures. This will certainly consolidate its position among most countries and races of the international community as the position of Polaris among stars, as mentioned by Confucius.

The ideal of the "kingly way," or benevolent governance, gradually developed by the Confucians during the following dynasties cannot but produce a positive effect on the foreign policy of modern China. Just and fair international communication and respect for the independent choices of national cultures in the "kingly way" of ancient China is comparable to the policy of support and coexistence of multiple civilizations in modern society.

The ideal of the "governance with virtue" of the Chinese people has not only a longstanding historical tradition but also a solid ethical foundation. As a personal philosophic and moral principle, the Confucian thought of "criticizing oneself more seriously, but criticizing others less seriously" meant to guide the behavior of the Chinese people. Such a personal ethic may be applied as an ethical guide to the political activities of any country. The rulers, from the emperor to the kings of all states, and then to officials at various posts should earnestly practice what they advocated and then taught the people around them to imitate their behavior. This personal ethical thought can also be used to instruct the political actions of a country, as Confucius said, "If the people of far-off lands do not submit, then the ruler must attract them by enhancing the prestige of his culture." This is similar to the new educational and enlightening principle of humanity in modern society to avoid forcing other people to copy one's own lifestyle, even though it may seem better and more humane than their original one. However, there is no reason to solve such problems by military force.

Of course, the ideal of the "governance with virtue" of Confucianism does not neglect or deny all wars. According to Confucius, a war can be initiated by the emperor alone to attack and control the kings who invade other states only for their own benefit. This is similar to a local war nowadays that is authorized only by the UN in order to settle some international conflicts. In ancient China the supreme power to initiate a war was exercised by the emperor himself, but at present the power is exercised by the Security Council of the UN according to a decision made by its members through a vote. The military duty may be assigned to some countries or to international organizations.

Because of the defects in the intelligence and morality of human beings, local wars and conflicts are difficult to avoid. However, in the modern "global village," with its members more closely linked, people must go beyond utilitarianism in the treatment of international relationships and step forward into a new era with peaceful, fair, and moral international relationships.

图书在版编目（CIP）数据

和平：中国人的文化根柢 / 吴根友著.

北京：外文出版社，2006

ISBN 978-7-119-04493-4

I.和…II.吴…III.和平共处—研究—中国—英文 IV.D820

中国版本图书馆 CIP 数据核字（2006）第 060622 号

策　　划：黄友义

责任编辑：胡开敏　杨春燕　刘芳念
英文翻译：郝光锋　梁发明　王　台
英文审定：Foster Stockwell　王明杰
印刷监制：张国祥

和平——中国人的文化根柢

吴根友　著

© 2007 外文出版社

出版发行：

外文出版社（中国北京百万庄大街 24 号）

邮政编码：100037　　http://www.flp.com.cn

电　　话：008610-68320579（总编室）

　　　　　008610-68995852（发行部）

　　　　　008610-68327750（版权部）

制　　版：

外文出版社照排中心

印　　制：

北京外文印刷厂

开本：787mm × 1092mm 1/16　印张：13

2007 年第 1 版第 1 次印刷

（英）

ISBN 978-7-119-04493-4

08800（平）

7-E-3726P

建议上架：

原版／对外汉语